I Want To Tell You

I Want To Tell You

by O. J. Simpson

My Response to
Your Letters, Your Messages,
Your Questions

LITTLE, BROWN AND COMPANY
Boston New York Toronto London

All of Mr. Simpson's proceeds from the sale of this book and any other rights associated with the publication of this work will be used to benefit Mr. Simpson's defense fund in the legal proceedings that are taking place in Los Angeles, California.

———————————

First Edition

ISBN 0-316-34100-2

10 9 8 7 6 5 4 3 2 1

RRD-VA

Published simultaneously in Canada by Little, Brown & Company (Canada) Limited

Printed in the United States of America

Contents

Foreword

This book began with 300,000 letters from men, women, and children of all ages, occupations, national and ethnic backgrounds, from all fifty states and many countries of the world, who chose to write to a man they had never met.

On June 17, 1994, millions of television viewers watched mesmerized as O.J. Simpson in a white Ford Bronco rode slowly down the Los Angeles freeways, followed by California Highway Patrol cars, to his unexpected date with destiny. This was the day that one of America's most popular and highly regarded public figures was charged with the murders of his ex-wife Nicole Brown Simpson and her friend Ronald Goldman and was due to surrender to the authorities. It did not happen as planned, of course, and speculation from law enforcement officials, the media, and O.J.'s closest associates ranged from thoughtful to outlandish throughout that astonishing afternoon and evening. In fact, O.J. Simpson went home, and from there into police custody, into the Los Angeles County Jail—and into the daily consciousness of the world community. Like millions of other Americans, I was one of those watching TV that night.

I had met O.J. twenty-five years earlier when I was a photographer for *Life* and *The Saturday Evening Post*. O.J., who had just finished his education at the University of Southern California, was embarking on his career with the Buffalo Bills, and he and his first wife, Marguerite, had purchased a simple Tudor-style suburban home on my block in the Bel Air Skycrest section of Los Angeles. My daughter, Suzanne, and my son Marc often tagged along as O.J. jogged backward through the hilly streets, and on Sunday mornings I sometimes watched as O.J. played tag football in the street with other neighborhood children.

Years later, our mutual friend Robert Kardashian asked me to direct a music video for his then-wife Kris's birthday and I met O.J. again, this time at his office where he sang new lyrics to Randy Newman's "I Love L.A." in honor of Kris. Now, twenty-five years later, like O.J., I too had changed my career. I was no longer a freelance journalist working for any news medium. For the last eighteen years I had been a producer and director of mini-series and motion pictures for television, and during these same years I had collaborated with Norman Mailer and Albert Goldman on several books, conducting in-depth interviews with the principal subjects for these writers.

In October of 1994, Robert Kardashian called me and said that I might be called as a material witness in O. J.'s case because of my past association with O.J. and that I would need to meet with him.

Our first meeting was on Halloween night, just as little ghosts, Power Rangers, and Princess Jasmines and their parents had begun ringing doorbells. Skip Taft, O.J.'s longtime friend and attorney, Robert, and I presented ourselves at the jail in downtown Los

Angeles. My name was on the court-approved list to see O.J. I stood beside them in a small, bare room.

We were immediately confronted with the standard walk-through metal detector much like those at airports. On the wall to the left, a sign warned attorneys that if they did not follow all the rules they would not be permitted to see their clients. Under this sign were smaller numbered rules listing items that could not be brought into the visiting area. Only then did I realize that this was not the area where friends and family visited prisoners, but a separate waiting room reserved for attorneys, investigators, and material witnesses.

My driver's license was checked against a list of approved visitors and I signed a form. We passed through the metal detector and the first sally port door. As that solid steel door clanged behind me—the steel-on-steel clamor and grind of that prison door slamming behind you is unsettling—I knew it was a sound of force telling you more powerfully than words that you're entering a world where you are not in control, where your every movement will be regimented by this iron and concrete institution. It is a sound of finality: you are inside, and everything free and familiar is outside.

Just then a second sally port door opened and we walked into a large pastel gray-blue room without windows, even more brightly lit than the room before. Directly ahead and on the right side were several rows of stools bolted to three long tables with glass partitions, while on the other side of the partitions were also rows of stools where inmates must sit while talking with those on the other side.

I followed Skip and Robert to the left. We walked past seven or eight rooms with their solid waist-high partitions topped by glass that rose to the ceiling. This was an unnaturally silent place with no hint of the cacophony and vibrancy of real life outside. It was spotlessly clean.

The last room, the largest, was split by a glass partition six feet long. On each side was a gray Formica flange that served as a table. Inch-thick glass rose almost three feet from this surface, topped by a metal lip. The room was open to the ceiling. The prisoner and his visitors could breathe the same air. Our side of the room held two chairs with chrome U-shaped frames and molded orange seats, design relics of the fifties. Robert reached into the adjoining room and took a chair for me, identical to the other two, setting it down at the partition that divided the room in half. For the next six or seven minutes, we sat waiting in the sterile quiet.

Then two sheriff's deputies appeared heading directly toward our glass room. O.J. walked slightly ahead of them. He was casual, with a little smile on his face as he looked around the large room at other prisoners being visited in the open area. His hands were loosely cuffed in front, a chain between them linking them to a metal belly restraint. He held a brown expandable file folder in his hands, the kind that usually has woven ties to secure the top flap. But, of course, there were no ties or laces on the folder now, nor any laces in his immaculate white high-top canvas shoes. He wore a blue prison jumpsuit with a U-neck, and where a handkerchief would have decorated a suit the words LA COUNTY JAIL were stenciled in white. Beneath the jumpsuit he wore a white T-shirt. He was clean shaven and his hair, while short, looked freshly groomed. He was calm, collected. Despite the jailhouse garb, he did not look like a man in prison.

One of the deputies handed the attorneys three books, which

O.J. had just finished reading, across the top of the glass: *Spencerville* by Nelson DeMille, *Deadly Rich* by Edward Stuart, and *The First Directorate* by Oleg Kalugin. The last caught my eye; it was the autobiography of a KBG agent whom I had met the previous year in Russia.

As O.J. sat down in the spotless orange chair opposite me, both his hands were uncuffed by a deputy. In a move that surprised me, O.J. reached down and attached one of the cuffs to a chain fastened to the floor. He did it with a unique grace and sudden smoothness—much the way he once would have surprised a lineman who thought he was about to tackle him. His eyes were sharp, intently alert, like an eagle. He had a total awareness of his surroundings just as he had once had on the football field or in the announcer's booth. I realized this sterile cubicle, five by eight feet in size, was now his only place for contact with the outside world where neither the state nor the news media could scrutinize him. This was O.J.'s new home. And while his body was chained from the waist to the floor, in this room, at this moment, he was, in his own way, a free man.

As soon as the deputies left and closed the glass door behind them, O.J. shook hands with us jail-style, a high-five met across the glass by Skip, Robert, and finally by me. Then he started talking to his attorneys.

As he spoke with Skip and Robert, I could tell by his body language what he thought of people being mentioned. The moment his lawyers uttered the name of someone he was unsure of, or mentioned a friend he felt had betrayed him, O.J.'s voice would develop an edge. Then a different person's name would come up—someone he liked—and his voice would soften, his firm posture would relax a little. O.J.

Simpson was not a man to hide his emotions.

After a few minutes I spoke for the first time. Robert introduced me, and reminded him of our prior meetings. When I mentioned to O.J. that my daughter, Suzanne, had baby-sat for him when Arnelle and Jason were young, he looked carefully at me for the first time. I reminded him of the night Suzanne had won $100 playing backgammon with him. My then-wife, Judi, told our daughter she could not keep the money—she had to spend it instead on presents for O.J.'s children. O.J. smiled and chuckled now. I think he even remembered Suzanne. At least he gave me the impression that he did. Our conversation moved to the subject of my being a material witness.

At the end of my first visit, I expected the guards to take O.J. away while we waited, but the routine was different. We left while he waited for the guards. I found his isolation at that moment curiously disturbing. Once I turned away, I could not look back.

As the sally port door opened, sending us back into a different world, I thought about O.J.'s cell and about the images of those he loved, and those he might cherish or dread. I did not look back. I feared that if I did, he would not be there.

That night, after I returned home, Robert called. He said that as he watched O.J. and me renew contact he was struck by how well we got along. Robert told me he had an idea for a book in which O.J. would respond to the 300,000 letters he had received since being jailed. He suggested I do a series of interviews with O.J. and fashion them into a book.

I visited O.J. the very next day. The routine of entering the jail was the same. But this time O.J. was already there and talking to

Robert and Skip.

Robert hooked up a tape recorder, sticking a bent paper clip into a small space between the glass and its metal frame to hang the microphone down on his side of the glass. O.J. leaned forward, looked me directly in the eyes and said, "Let's start."

What came forth was a flood of words. Before Robert could even get the tape going, O.J. was talking, telling me of his innocence, his emotional state, recent events, his whole life. Although there were four of us in that glass room, for those moments the others did not exist for him. He spoke so quickly, like torrents cascading from a ruptured dam, that I soon had to interrupt him and try to channel his thoughts. I had questions to ask, a briefcase full of them. I had dozens of topics to try to cover in this first interview and in the many that would follow.

It was hard work for O.J. His mind wandered—there were so many letters, so many issues, so much he wanted to say, and a few matters on which he could say nothing because of his pending trial. Later, reading the transcripts of the interviews, I could see that he had answered the questions, not in neat numbered paragraphs, but in a kaleidoscope of anguish and emotion. It was obvious that he knew from the letters he had read what people wanted to know, and he knew, very clearly, what he wanted to say to them. He spoke from the heart, never cautioned or censored by his attorneys, or asking to go back and change an answer.

As I sat with O.J. in this glass room, I soon realized that he could not discuss his ex-wife's death or its effect on his children's lives in any detail without losing his composure. Sometimes there was only the sound of his sobbing and the muffled speech of other prisoners and their visitors. In these moments, even though I was only two feet away, he was alone. This is the room where he spends every minute he can when not in court or sleeping. He is allowed visitors on Monday through Thursday from the early morning until 7:50 p.m., as many as five people at a time. He is always watched by a deputy sheriff just outside this glass room. On most days, he sees his attorneys with witnesses, which include his family and loved ones. On Friday through Sunday he is visited in another part of the jail.

I noticed the clock. We had spoken this time for almost two hours. The time limit bore down on us and I interrupted him to explain we would have to leave soon but that I would be back. We would meet again until we had completed his book and answered those letters. I would make nine more trips to visit him. Sometimes he would be elated or deeply distressed after just talking by phone to his younger children. Each visit gave me another view of this extraordinary man. There were times when he was depressed because of what had happened in court that day, or jovial when his older children came to see him. In each interview I seemed to find a different man, but one who was ultimately optimistic, reflective, and introspective. Each time as I left, as the sally port door opened to free me from the confinement of the jail, I reflected on my first visit with O.J. I remembered my fear that if I looked back at him, he would not be there.

Lawrence Schiller
Los Angeles
December 1994

*This book is dedicated
to all the people who brought love into my life.*

*And a special thanks to Burt,
who was the inspiration for this book.*

O.J.

Fame is a vapor;

Popularity an accident,

   and money takes wing;

And those who cheer today

   will curse tomorrow.

The only thing that

   endures—is character.

———————————

Words that I've

tried to live by.

O.J.

Part 1

I Always Answer
My Mail

I have been accused of the crime of murder, a double murder. The State of California charged me on June 17, 1994, with the deaths of my former wife Nicole Brown Simpson and Ronald Goldman, and arrested me later that same day. Since the day of my arrest I have had to defend myself not only in court but in the eyes of the public and the news media. In this book I am speaking publicly for the first time since my arrest, for two reasons.

First and foremost, I want to respond to the more than 300,000 people who wrote to me. I want to say thank you, I want to tell you those letters were a godsend. People wrote not only in the United States but from all over the world. Their letters started coming right after my arrest. Most were supportive, most of them gave me hope — all of them made me feel still part of the world. I first heard about my mail when a female deputy sheriff, on my second day in jail, said, "We've got a problem. We've got too many letters for you." They had received more letters for me in one day than they had for all the other prisoners, some 6,000 prisoners, at the Los Angeles County Jail.

In my spare eight by five foot cell there were just bundles of mail, big bundles, small bundles. I remember all that mail around my feet. It was wonderful, the one thing in my life at that moment that was wonderful and beautiful. The jail's phone was ringing off the hook with people asking for my booking number, 4013970, so that their letters would get to me. They had to hire more people at the jail to help them with my mail. Here I was, still in a fog, and one of the lieutenants comes to me and wants to discuss the problem of my mail! Letters were coming to Los Angeles without any address, some just said "O.J. Simpson, L.A. Jail." It just did not stop. One writer, Susan Geise, from Yorba Linda, California, said I needed my own ZIP code.

Thank you. To everyone who wrote, thank you. Your letters kept me sane in those first days.

Some of the people who wrote letters to me didn't know me and really hadn't followed my career. But I had made an impression on them and whatever they remembered about me was good and happy and honest. There was a letter from a woman who said she had an image of me as a positive and good person. She said she was writing because she "just cared." During those first nights in jail I was so depressed, not only about what was going on with me, but imagining the pain of Nicole, the loss of Nicole. I was hurting, I was hurting real bad — the worst pain of my life. Some of the letters validated what my mother was telling me over and over, that the Lord was really forging me for something else, something better. Other letters said I had the attention of all football fans, but now my forum was more than just a sports arena.

Dear O.J.,

I have nothing but the greatest respect and admiration for all that you have been able to accomplish. All of the strength and determination that got you to this point in your career today will also help get you through these tough times that you are now facing. There are so many, many people pulling for you. All of us believe in you and love you, and we hope that maybe you can gain some strength from us to help give you the strength to get through this horrible time.

My thoughts and prayers are with you each day.

Always a fan,

Linda Keifer
Boise, ID

Dear Juice:

How are you?
I am convinced that your life has been meaningful. How about you? As you look at your life what are you most proud of? Your accomplishments as an athlete are many, but I imagine that in the context of your life there

are other things much more important to you. What are they?

You are in my prayers every night asking the Lord to give you grace and strength in these days. Please keep in your heart and soul the knowledge that there are many of us who stand with you no matter what. Until next time, my friend. Vaya con Dios.

Sincerely,

Howie Alford
Livermore, CA

Dear O.J.:

I know that deep black bottomless pit you live with everyday. Now, it is even blacker & deeper than anyone can imagine, unless you have experienced it personally.

O.J., I cry for you in your despair, I cry for you in your loss of your wife, I cry for your crucifixion.

I am not a sports fan. I write to you as a person who has touched the same depths of despair, who has come through the other side, but can still remember the daily hell.

O.J., call on our higher power, even if you feel He's so far away right now, ask your guardian angels to guide you through this, the most trying time of your life.

   Believe in yourself, one day at a time, one hour at a time, if that's what it takes.

Most sincerely,

Betty Chappell
Aurora, Ontario, Canada

Days later, after I had read hundreds and hundreds of letters, I started reading between the lines and realized that there were so many people hurting out there. Maybe not to the degree I was — the loss of Nicole, the pain of Nicole, never left my mind as I read the letters. But the one thing that also came across loud and clear was that there were a lot of people in pain out there. I could hear their fear, their hopelessness, their sadness. I knew I was not alone. From these letters I started to find support. These first letters were sort of the only security blanket I had. I started coming out of the fog I'd been in since I was first jailed.

Dear O.J.,

   I just wanted you to know millions of people are thinking of you, and praying for you and your family.

Take one day at a time. Maybe someday I'll get a note from you, that'll make my day for the rest of my days. Goodnight, O.J., take care.

God Bless You.

Rosie Conover
Sunnyvale, CA

———

Another letter told me I can't worry about yesterday and I can't get wrapped up in the apprehensions of what might happen tomorrow. I have learned in here you have to deal with the day for itself alone. In this jail you've got to deal with each day. Life in here is tough. These letters showed someone was paying attention, understanding my situation. All these letters justified the efforts I had made throughout my life. I felt I had earned their support.

I have asked myself why so many people wrote. If I had just been arrested routinely, maybe the writers would have thought it was wrong to write or needless. If it hadn't been for the ride to my home in my friend A.C.'s—Allen Cowlings's— Bronco on that June Friday, I think many people would not have witnessed the desperate place I was in. It's amazing to me how many people felt the frustration or the pain that I was feeling. Many of those who wrote did not comment on my guilt or innocence. They just said that what they saw in me was pure pain. That day I just wanted to end the pain. I believe the public saw beyond what was wrongly described in the press as the "white Bronco chase." I found there were people out there who appreciated the way I have lived my life. These writers said I had not always been perfect, but they knew I'd never maliciously done anything wrong.

I started to answer some of my mail. I soon discovered that it was just about impossible to personally answer the tens of thousands of letters I was receiving. I gave mail to Cathy Randa, my assistant for the last twenty years, and she started to sort the letters. I thanked little children who sent dollars and coins from their allowances, and returned the money where there was a return address. In just a few days there were more letters than even Cathy could hope to manage so she recruited help. Volunteers started to read the mail and I was given letters each and every day when I was visited in jail by my attorney Nicole Pulvers, or by Cathy. Over ninety-six percent of the letters were positive in nature. The majority of the letters have some religious theme to them. Many addressed important social issues that need to be dealt with. There was obviously a small minority of racist letters, many of them unsigned.

Dear O.J.,

    Could you ask someone, like Rosie [Grier], to drop me a note or call if my letters are making your life better in any way? I need to know that the efforts I'm putting out are not in vain.

Valerie Summers
San Diego, CA

Several months later Robert suggested that I write this book as a way of answering all of the letters. I really wanted to answer each and every one, good, bad, and indifferent, but it is just impossible. I would prefer, actually, to talk to the people who wrote, to call them on the phone or speak to them in person. I hope that everyone who wrote to me will find, somewhere in this book, a response to the thoughts and feelings they expressed in their letters to me. That is the first reason for this book.

The second reason is financial. Many people think that I am very rich and have access to unlimited funds. This is not the case. I have succeeded and have been able to provide for my family, friends, and loved ones. Some say that I have been too generous at times. The legal system requires that I defend myself in a trial since my statements that I am "one hundred percent not guilty" have not been accepted by the District Attorney of Los Angeles County. This has and will continue to consume all of my resources. When the system starts to gain speed, one must keep up with it or be run over. The State of California has unlimited resources—from the taxpayer—to prosecute me. These resources will never run out so long as taxes are paid and the state wishes to proceed. I do not have access to similar funds to prove my innocence. In fact, I do not have the sort of sums that many people seem to think I have. I am using all my financial resources, and I am now in need of additional funds for my defense. I have asked the writers of the letters included here to contribute their letters, with an explanation that the income derived from this book will go to my defense fund. I do want the readers to know that I have provided for my children in any event.

I am grateful that even those who believe in my guilt also believe that I should have my day in court and have agreed to let their words be published in this book.

One Hundred Percent Not Guilty

The incredible effrontery of your "100% not guilty"
lie boggles the imagination. A chronic wife beater,
coming from a violent "sport" earning obscene money,
is a pathetic excuse for a man. Now there's enough
circumstantial evidence to convict a dozen people.
Get off our backs with your expensive lawyers trading on
your celebrity. This circus costs us taxpayers too much.
See the light & plea bargain.

Helen Stanton
Los Angeles, CA

I am one hundred percent not guilty. In my open letter read on television on June 17, 1994, by my friend Robert Kardashian, I said I was innocent.

When asked at my arraignment, where the charges against me were first formally stated in court, I said, "I am one hundred percent not guilty." I said it again in Judge Ito's chambers and I say it again here. I will continue to speak this truth until the day I die.

Ms. Stanton, like the writers of some other letters I received (not all of them unsigned), believes I am guilty. And some people who represent the State of California don't believe that I am innocent. So I am forced to put my life before a jury and live with their decision. It is easy to make rumors and speculations and news reports fit a preconceived idea. It's difficult to erase those rumors and speculations from people's minds.

Dear O.J.,

Please say it's not true. Please say you didn't kill that woman like that.

My friends all think you did it but I don't believe them. I believe you, O.J.

[Anonymous]
Postmark: Goldsboro, NC

To: O.J. Simpson

You scumbag and coward.
You should have shot yourself in the Bronco — Coward!
Beating up on women and killing two unarmed people in

your selfish rage. You will undoubtedly "get off" but that's ok—save room for the wrath of God. And one day your children will know who took their mother away.

I am just an average middle aged housewife (white) with a wonderful (black) husband of 12 years.

[Anonymous]
Postmark: Van Nuys, CA

This is my first letter — ever — to a celebrity.

I want to state unequivocally that I did not commit these horrible crimes. I loved Nicole, I could never do such a thing. I don't think I even know anyone who's capable of doing such things. I can't think of anybody I've ever known who could have done something this terrible.

I have tried all my life to be a good citizen. I was brought up "to do unto others as you would have others do unto you." Now I see how fickle it can be out there, how quickly some people are ready to judge and want me to be guilty. It appeared to me, at least with the press, that they wanted to believe only in my guilt. That's what I think may have hurt me the most in the beginning.

How could anybody say I could kill this woman? How can anybody say that? Don't they understand that I'd jump in front of a bullet for Nicole? That I'd jump in front of a train to protect my family, to protect any member of Nicole's family?

Trust me, I never would have taken Nicole from our two little children. I would have taken myself out of their lives, not Nicole out of their lives.

I can't relate to why anybody would kill another person. I certainly can't relate to why someone would kill Nicole and Mr. Goldman. I have sat in my jail cell and asked myself what I would say to whoever did this horrible crime. The only thing I can think of is "Why?"

I also have asked myself: Can I forgive whoever killed Nicole? My Bible tells me I have to. Right now I can't. But I know whoever did it is going to have to face the Lord one day.

Dear O.J.:

If you are innocent don't give up! You have four children that need you more than anything. Pray to whatever God you believe in. I know that the media has crucified you but you're not dead and as long as you have breath in your lungs, breathe.

You're stronger than you think and forget about the MEDIA.

Sincerely,

Pamela Howard
Neptune City, NJ

When the jury finds me innocent, when the evidence shows I am innocent and I am set free, I wonder whether the public will ever accept my innocence. I don't think some people will. Sometimes I think that the only way I can ever deal with that is to tell myself I don't care. But I do care because I have family. I have kids. I do care.

I know I have one chance of total vindication. One chance. And that is for the police to catch who did it, or for the killers to come forward. I think that once I'm vindicated in court, the police's attention must turn to finding the real killers.

I have no doubt that eventually they will catch them, probably because of something else they did. Eventually we are going to find out who did it. I have no doubt in my mind. It might be five years from now, it might be ten years from now. I have no doubt.

Nicole Simpson

Dear Mr. Simpson:

As I write, I must first offer my sympathy to you and the Simpson family, the Brown family, and the Goldman family.

God knows, whereas you may or may not know what happened that awful night.

Faith and peace to you.

Willa M. Stamps
Diamond Bar, CA

Dear Mr. O.J. Simpson,

I write this letter to let you know that God loves you and I do too. I'm very sorry about the death of your ex-wife and Mr. Goldman. My prayers have been that

God will sustain her family, the children and the family
of the other victim.

My love and prayers,

Brenda F. Miller
Boynton Beach, FL

I now pray at night before I go to bed. And then I dream. I dream almost every night. God brings Nicole to me in my dreams. She's radiant. Complete loveliness. Sometimes I see the house that I was going to build in Cabo San Lucas. This house is almost perfect in my dream and we are playing in it and stuff, Nicole and me. And when I wake up it's like I want to die sometimes.

God has brought Nicole to me in my dreams. It is never the past that I visit in my dreams. That only takes place when I am conscious and awake. Only during the day do I think of our past together and not the future. Now when He brings Nicole to me it is for something that we had wanted to do or something that we were going to do.

One night, in my dreams, Sydney was grown up and getting married. Nicole and I were together in our back yard on Rockingham Avenue in Brentwood where we got married. But now, in my dream, Sydney was in Nicole's wedding dress and she was the one getting married there.

Interviewer: O.J. started to choke up and then wept open-
ly as he spoke about these dreams. His head dropped into
his hands and he slumped forward, burying his face
between his knees. He began again to speak of his
daughter, who now could never have a wedding with both
parents looking on proudly.

He lifted his head and started talking softly about the
house in Cabo San Lucas.

I had some land in Cabo, at the tip of the Baja Peninsula in
Mexico, a big lot I was going to build on. Nicole also loved the
beach, the sea, and there is a golf course just around the corner.
During that last year when we came back together, we were just
beginning to talk to designers, and one guy had even made up
a mock design. He had drawn little sketches and so forth. The
house was basically going to be open and airy, plenty of room
to entertain friends. This was another part of my dream that
cannot come true.

Now I can only look at the house on Rockingham Avenue. It
was something that Nicole and I had created, something that
was a part of us and even more centered on us, because it was
before we had kids. I mean, out of our love, we made this house
that represented our dreams then and the dreams we were going
to have. The feeling you have when you come onto our property is that it is something that grew out of our love for one
another. It reflects what we wanted for our kids. It began in
the time before Sydney and Justin were born, when our world
was just Nicole and me. Now it's the only thing left of us that

we created together for our kids. We had the front yard redesigned so the kids had a play area to themselves, so they could be watched from the kitchen. The pool area was also rebuilt. Everything was done over. This house is going to be hard for me to give up because of the thought that someone else will have something so personal, will change it, most likely. I want my kids to grow up and appreciate this home because it is the last tangible connection they have to their mother and me together. I know every time I hug the kids, especially Sydney, I'm hugging Nicole, for before Sydney and Justin there was just Nicole.

Dear O.J.,

> *Your daughter is very pretty and is very attached to you. I've seen how she gave you a kiss at the burial. She's very smart so no matter what anyone tells her she knows that something is not right. Your youngest boy is very close to his sister. She will guide him through these bad times, and will help him through all this ordeal.*
>
> *God bless you, O.J.*
>
> *Nancy Barbosa*
> *Brooklyn, NY*

Dear Mr. O.J.

My name is Marcus and I'm 8 yrs old. I know you didn't kill your wife, because you loved her very much. Will think of you in our prayers. I wished your son lived in San Francisco so I could make him laugh and not worry to much.

Marcus Parish
San Francisco, CA

I wish that too. Halloween was a special time, we loved the costumes at Halloween. I'm never going to be able to go trick-or-treating again with my kids and their mother. I'm never going to hear Sydney and Justin say the words "Mommy, Mommy." I'm never going to hear those words come out of my kids' mouths again, never again. Sometimes, when I remember those days, I find myself crying.

I wonder sometimes what Nicole was thinking at the end. I think now about what must have been going through her head when she realized what was about to happen to her, oh man. It hurts me to think about it. I would have put up a fight, I would have protected Nicole, you know. I'll never hear my kids say "Mommy" again. That hurts me every day. I know it hurts my kids, too.

Mr. Simpson,

I am writing to express my sympathy for the death of your ex-wife and the mother of your children. They are the real victims here. Not only have they lost their mother but it was the way it happened. If you had anything to do with that then you should take your punishment. If not, then the public and the media should leave you alone.

You are innocent until proven guilty in a court of law.

Good Luck to you and you and your children are in my prayers.

Sincerely,
Linda Davis
East Peoria, IL

I could never kill anyone, especially Nicole. How could I deprive my kids of a mother. How could I look them in the eyes every day. I couldn't do that. I could never do that! It's got to be horrible, just horrible for my children to lose their mother and not have me there to comfort them.

Hi, O.J.,

I believe that you loved Nicole very much and that you feel you have lost perhaps your best friend. Sometimes our greatest "sin" is caring too much for someone, being in the wrong place at the wrong time, and/or not implementing ways to avoid and abstain from that which could cause the most harm. Someone today mentioned "the victims" as though the two deceased people were the

only victims. I believe that you, too, have been and will
continue to be a victim.

God bless you and
your children.

[Unsigned]
Postmark: Toledo, OH

I ask myself, What could I have changed? Would my destiny have changed? I think back to the time when I had no problems. The world was my oyster. We had two beautiful kids and my wife was gorgeous. In 1985, I married Nicole after knowing her for more than seven years. I loved the life that we were living. We traveled and we were in love. I was at peace with who I was and what I was. Nicole had so much patience with me. Like every person, Nicole had her faults. She blamed other people for her problems when she was unhappy. But the way she treated our kids when they were born, that made up for all the rest of it.

Nicole was a very caring mother. She never left the children. I worked sometimes in New York for half the year when I was with NBC. I was never concerned about my kids because I knew they were in Nicole's hands. I had one thousand percent faith and trust in Nicole's decisions about the kids. I was in shock when she asked for the separation in January of 1992. Nicole soon after filed for divorce. Our divorce became final on October 25, 1992.

Maybe if we each had been more open in our relationship, if we had been more spiritual together, we would have stayed together. When we were married, we would take the kids to church occasionally, maybe every week, sometimes once a month. When we went to church, we didn't share the words with each other. We did the right thing by going, by taking the kids, but that wasn't enough. I was like Nicole: you go to church to feel good that you're in church, then you take the kids to the beach, or bowling. You think you are doing the right thing. But I can say we didn't share the word of God with one another. We never took God and put Him in our relationship.

_____

Hi, O.J.!

Keep your head up high!
When I wake in the night and think of you and pray for you, I know you are hurting more deeply than you can ever express to anyone, nor could anyone fully understand the hurt. Deep down you know you are not alone. You know who is always with you, don't you, O.J.? You have a gentleness about you that even you seem to be unaware of.
Live, and may your special prayers be answered.

Margaret Daniel
Garden Grove, CA

_____

I held it against my father for a lot of years after he separated from my mother. Then, when I separated from my first wife, Marquerite, I realized it wasn't necessarily my dad's fault that he and my mom broke up. Sometimes two people reach a point when it's time to go down different paths. That's what happened to Nicole and me even before were divorced.

I know Nicole had to go through whatever she was going through. Many women who have kids in their twenties go through changes. Once they get to their thirties they need to discover their own identity. These women need to go out and make their own friends and do their own thing. When Nicole and I split up that first time in January of '92, it caused us both a lot of pain.

It took a little time, but after Nicole and I separated I became comfortable with myself, comfortable with being alone. I was happy and I was content. I really didn't need to be involved with anyone. Then, three months later, I started seeing Paula Barbieri. Paula, a beautiful model, allowed me a lot of freedom because she had a professional life of her own and we both had full lives. And Paula's a very spiritual person.

Then Nicole and I got back together in '93. I didn't know what her motivation was for wanting us to get back together. I loved the time I spent with her and the kids. I committed to a year. Nicole became my girlfriend again and we practically started calling each other husband and wife.

I split up with Paula. I hurt Paula a lot. I committed to that one year and Nicole and I started going steady again.

Dear O.J.,

I know at this time you feel everything is gone and you have no way out. May I say how I feel about

Destiny — because no human being has control over his or her life. Life was given to us, a blessed gift from Jesus Christ. The most amazing thing about this, God will come and collect what belongs to Him. All of us are the sheep that belong to the shepherd.

I am among the many mothers praying and wishing the best for you.

Love, Another Mom,

Glendle L. Williams
Dallas, TX

Destiny. Maybe when I committed to that year of going steady Nicole should have moved back into our home on Rockingham. But I didn't want our kids moving back in my house one month and having to move out one month later.

You don't do that to kids.

Dear O.J.,

First, you don't know me, my name is Tommy Montgomery. I wish there was something I could do to help you.

There can be nothing more tragic than for your children to lose their mother as well as their father at the same time. I hope they catch the people who really committed these atrocities.

You are in my prayers and those of everyone I know.

Your Friend,

Tommy Montgomery
Huntsville, AL

Looking at my own life, I think mothers are even more important than fathers. My mother raised me after my father left when I was four. There was nobody more important than my mom. But every child has a father. There comes a day when they need each other. That day came with me, too. I was lucky: Nicole loved my father. They got along so well. They laughed a lot. My dad was always trying to teach her to cook, especially his type of macaroni and cheese, which was brown and crispy on the top. He was a great chef. He taught her to cook all types of cornbreads. Sometimes he came down from San Francisco just to cook dinner and show Nicole something new. They were always in the kitchen laughing together. In many ways Nicole's relationship with my dad was probably better than my relationship with my dad. I just know when they spent time together both of them enjoyed every minute of it.

Nicole's family adopted me, too, and I adopted them. I treated her family every bit as good as I treated my own family. I had so much respect for Nicole's mother, Judy. She's understanding and giving. In the last four years I would talk to Judy more than anybody else in the Brown family. I was so close to Judy that I talked to her more than Nicole did. Through Nicole's mother I tried to understand Nicole. I tried to find answers to what Nicole may have been dealing with, or going through, what was weighing on Nicole that she couldn't express to me.

Dear O.J.,

I am writing this letter to you hoping in some small way it will bring you some comfort. I know it has got to be hard, trying to adjust to that small place called a cell. My heart goes out to your family, especially your mother.

My heart also goes out to Nicole's and Ronald's families in their hour of need. I pray that the Lord will give them strength to go on with their lives.

I hope you will be able to find some peace and get some sleep while you are there.

Pat Malloy
Anchorage, AK

One of the toughest parts of what's happening to me now is that I loved Nicole and I need to share the memory of my love for Nicole. I shared what I felt for Nicole the most in the past with her mother and now I can't talk to her. Judy is the type of person who can't talk unless she can give her all and I know she can't just now. I thought about writing to Judy, but I can't. Her loss may be even greater than mine. It would be too difficult for both of us. When I call Sydney and Justin at Judy and Lou's, where they are now living, I sometimes get Lou. I've expressed to him how it really hurts me not being able to share Nicole with Judy. I feel that Lou represents the family and he has said, in so many words, "Let the legal system handle it." Nicole had three sisters: her oldest sister, Denise; Dominique, who is called Minnie, was younger than Nicole; and Tanya was the youngest. There was lots of sibling rivalry, especially between Denise and Nicole, but this is not the place to discuss it.

Just like there are issues I need to resolve with the Browns, I feel in me that I have so many unresolved issues with Nicole that I'll never be able to resolve with her now that she's gone. Sitting here in jail, I feel that I've been denied the right to properly mourn.

I was consulted about the funeral. I had my views on where Nicole should have been buried, but the Browns made the final decision. But, in fact, the cemetery was down in Laguna Beach where they live, an hour and a half from where we lived in Brentwood. That's all right for now, when Sydney and Justin live with the Browns, but in the future when this is all over and the kids are back with me, Sydney and Justin should have more access to their mother. That's the way it will be: I'll have the kids, and through them I'll still have some part of Nicole.

If I hadn't been a suspect at that time, I would have stepped in and had Nicole buried in Los Angeles. It wasn't that I was left out, or not consulted. I was, but I couldn't even think about it. I was hurting too much. Even if I wasn't a suspect, I would have had a real tough time making any kind of decisions at that moment.

Dear Mr. Simpson:

> *When an emotional injury*
> *takes place, the mind begins*
> *a process as natural as the*
> *healing of a physical wound.*
> *Let the process happen.*
> *Know that the pain will pass*
> *and, when it passes, you will be stronger,*
> *happier, more sensitive and aware.*

> *Leonard C. Harris, M.D.*
> *Hagerstown, MD*

I still have to mourn her. Every time I dip into it here in jail, it's too tough, it's too tough. It just takes everything I have just to survive here day to day, emotionally, you know. I don't want to be overly dramatic but I still have a lot of grieving that I just can't deal with here.

Pictures I Love

We always went to Hawaii for our winter vacation in the sun. Here Nicole is with Sydney, who is just three months old. As the years went on we took the entire family, and our group of friends on the islands became larger and larger. We stayed at the Kahala Hilton Hotel on the island of Oahu.

Here we are about to board the famous Orient Express. This was one of the great trips Nicole and I took—we went to Rome, Florence, and then back to London. The picture of us in shorts was taken in Monte Carlo where I went for a tennis tournament. I intended to win, but didn't.

The photograph on the left was kept in our bedroom. It was taken on our wedding day, February 2, 1985, in the backyard of our home where we were married. This delightful picture of Nicole and Justin was taken in Aspen when he had just learned to ski. Skiing was something we would do as a family and we all loved it.

The photograph on the left was taken at Christmastime in Aspen, Colorado. This trip was my present to the family. The picture above was also taken in Aspen, but before we had the children. It's in a little condo we rented. Some years we took our family and friends. We tried to never miss a year.

Paula doesn't look very spiritual in this picture, but she sure is. This photograph was taken at her mom's home last year and is one of my favorites.

Unknown Soldier

Dear O.J.,

    I read that you are tormented about the death of your ex-wife. I would be also. I am sure you cry for her. Do you also cry for Mr. Goldman?

[Unsigned]
Postmark: Boston, MA

I feel badly for Mr. Goldman's family. I feel his family's hurt and pain; but I had nothing to do with his death.

    To me he is like the unknown soldier, courageous.

Kids

A Shining Star

A shining star has fallen,
And in his eyes I see,
A man who once was there,
But no longer will he be.

My heart continues breaking,
With every tear you cry.
I steady feel your pain,
With every sigh you sigh.

I'm reaching out to you,
And my words, they are sincere.
If it's me you don't remember,
Please hold my poem dear.

A shining star has fallen,
Needing a friend indeed.
I am here to let you know,
You have a friend in me.

Every word you've read is true. Hope you like it, I wrote it
just now, for you.

Remember…you may have fallen to them, but to me, you're still shining!

> *Your new friend,*
> *Jamie B. Brown, Age 15*
> *Bakersfield, CA*

Some of the letters I have read over and over. When I received this poem, I tried to express to my assistant, Cathy Randa, that this is what bolsters me. This poem was just wonderful. And to think it was written by a fifteen-year-old. These kids, these people, are unbelievable. There are so many of these generous people out there. For a person, a kid, to take that time to do this, it shows me people really care. My friends who are witnesses have come to see me in jail and they say, "Juice, don't listen to these so-called opinion polls, don't listen to what they're saying in the press, it's the people who count."

I remember looking at the "letters to the editor" column, looking at the editorial page of the paper, the sports page in any paper, there's always somebody complaining about something. It's rare that you read somebody just talking about what's good. Because it's a natural human disposition to complain. When they're mad at something, people start to write, because they care. People started to write me because they cared and they were mad. They were mad at what they were hearing. They were paying attention to what was being said.

I kind of remember writing my first letter as a kid. I'm sure my first letter was to Santa Claus. I wanted a bicycle, I wanted a Higgins, a J.C. Higgins bike. I knew that Santa wasn't going to write back, he had too many letters coming to him. It's like me with all these letters, but I'm not Santa Claus. I didn't wait for Santa's letter, I just waited for my bicycle and I got a red one. A letter is now as important to me as a bicycle was then. Now I get all these letters from kids. They're writing to me — eleven-year-olds, five-years-olds, seven-year-olds, entire school classes of kids.

Dear Mr. O.J. Simpson:

We are a class of 7/8 grade students. Some of the class believes that you are innocent. Don't worry about all the pressure that is on you, because if you believe in God you will go to heaven. We all do admire all that you have done in the past — your football career, your help with charity, your fascinating endorsements, and your broadcasting career. Even if you are sentenced to life, when you die and if you believe in Jesus your spiritual life will still be alive. We also pray for you and your family.

Sincerely,

7/8 grade class of Trinity
Lutheran School
Redding, CA

Jacy C. Krogh, Justin Krogh,
Jason Collins, and the rest of
the class.

Dear O.J. "Juice" Simpson:

I know you didn't kill Nicole Brown Simpson and Ronald Goldman. I'm a big fan of yours when you played for the 49er's. Will you please send me a autograph card when you played for the 49er's. I am 11 years old.

Justin Caudill
Rialto, CA

Dear O.J.,

Hi! I am 12 years old and I am a fan of yours. I hope you will accept this letter to add to your other million or so. I don't think you killed Nicole or Ronald. Even if you did, I would still be your fan and so would my mom because everyone makes mistakes. We learned (from watching T.V. about you) that no one has privacy because the media puts their noses in everybody's bisness.

You know what? A program you made for kids at school to watch had your part tooken out but the kids refused to watch the program till your part was put back in. They put your part back in too.

Sincerely,

Lisa Miranda
Anaheim, CA

P.S. It is so unfair to see some nice, funny and innocent person (you) in jail.

When I received this letter from Lisa Miranda, I felt the kid's heart was in the right place. But what I did not like about this letter (and some others) was the part: "Even if you did it, I would still be your fan and so would my mom because everyone make mistakes." Obviously I thank Lisa for believing I am innocent, which I say, again, that I am. It's heartwarming to know the child has the ability to communicate her feelings. But it disturbs me that a kid would write about any kind of killing. It's something that shouldn't be brought into their lives. I know TV is there and you can't escape the effect of the media. But there's where parents need to step in.

If these were my children writing a letter to someone they had seen on TV who had been accused of committing a crime, any crime, I would hope my children would come to me and say they wanted to write down their thoughts in a letter. I think to be very open is good. It would be bad for them to keep all this inside themselves. But then, I would sit down and have a long talk with my kids and ask them why they're writing the letter. I would want them to understand in their hearts why they're writing. If my children said they saw this person on TV, and he was or had been their hero, and their hero had been accused of a crime, or had even been judged guilty of committing the crime, I would say to my kids, as I say to the children who write to me: "What makes me your hero? Let's take a look at what that is." I would say: "As a football player, it's quite all right to still view me, or my style of playing, as something that you'd like to do the way I do." But I would also say: "Let's not confuse the past with the other new issues." If I was in fact the perpetrator of this crime, which I'm not, I would also say: "This is someone that you shouldn't emulate." I might not use those exact words, but that is basically what I would say. Parents need to teach their kids how to understand their feelings, which feeling are positive, which feelings are negative, and how to control these feelings. I know sometimes young children can't differentiate one strong emotion from another, but that is where the parents need to step in. It's important for the kids who write to understand why they feel the way they do.

Dear O.J.

I am 6 year old. I love you—you did not do it. I pray for you.

Aaron Carrillo, Godbless
Orlando, FL

Dear O.J.

I hope you get out of Jail soon. I think you are innocent.

Your friend.
Spencer Harbin, Age 7
Anthony, KS

Now that I look back and think about it, I was never a big letter writer. When I was a kid I don't remember ever writing to anyone to console them about a tragic event, or the death of a loved one. As an adult, quite often I have written such letters. As a kid, I would be more likely to go by and see someone. I do remember the first time I was faced with the death of someone who was not a relative. This little girl in our neighborhood died when I was probably about seven or eight, and I went to her house with some food my mother made. In the projects, you get to know everybody and when there's a death in the neighborhood you go and you sit around. You just all sit around together.

The deaths that really stayed with me are those among my family and close friends. My grandmother and grandfather died when I was about Sydney's age. I think it is easier somehow to handle these things at a young age. I know that the first death that really got to me was my uncle Hollis. He lived with my mother, and he was the youngest of my grandparents' kids. He used to tell stories about the war to me and my older brother, Truman. We used to love sitting around Uncle Hollis while he told us stories about being in the army and how they — I think it was in Korea — how they had these flame-throwers and they had to blow them into these hillside caves. My uncle told us how he could hear these guys hiding in the caves screaming. It was horrible. But it was exciting to be close to my uncle.

Dear O.J.

Hi my name is Betsy Neal and I am 10 years old. I live in New York. I'm not writing just because I want to. I am because I care for you. Everyday I wonder if you did it or not. But I always pray that you didn't do it.

I know it is hard for you. If you did do it I will still care for you.

*your friend,
Betsy Neal
Fulton, NY*

Some writers of letters and a lot of kids don't seem to care if I'm guilty or innocent. They just want to believe in me. As I've said before, that's not right. What I have to say to these kids is that you must always accept responsibility for yourself. I say you have to believe in yourself first, you have to have God in you, and with God in you, you will have goodness in you.

I don't believe kids should try to emulate any person's style. It may be the in thing to do, but they have to develop their own style. It has to originate from within. You have to take responsibility for yourself. When I speak to kids, I say that you have to accept responsibility for your own actions. You can't blame your teachers; you can't say: "The teacher doesn't like me and that's why I didn't get a good grade," or "I didn't make the team because the coach's son plays the same position." I have always said and I say it again: You are handicapping yourself when you accept excuses. I say to everybody that if I had committed this crime, I would have had to take responsibility for my actions and I would have.

Dear O.J.

I am glad you didn't commit suicide because you have

to come back and be the honorary captain for the Bills when they make it to the Super Bowl next year. Plus, when the jury finds you not guilty, you have to do another Naked Gun movie (the Naked Gun movies are my favorite). O.J., I know and everybody knows you didn't kill your wife, you're too nice. In Ringwood everybody's cheering for ya and I'm sure everybody in the world is cheering for ya.

O.J., I'm praying for ya because you're the best. Even though I'm 13, I know when I see a great guy, you're great.

From your pal,

James Sanford
Ringwood, NJ

P.S. I've enclosed my allowance for the week, $5.00.

It's unbelievable that a kid would send his allowance. Thanks, James, but I don't feel comfortable taking your allowance. That's obviously something I don't do. What I am saying is that I can see James's heart, but to send me his allowance is just not right. I've instructed Cathy that she should send all the allowances back. If an adult makes the decision to send some money for my defense fund, that's one thing. But a kid, his allowance goes back.

I can't even keep pictures of my family in my cell. It's not because I'm not allowed to. I am. I just can't have a picture of my younger kids, Sydney and Justin, because it is so — it's all so debilitating for me when I see a picture of them. I can't control my emotions. I cry. I pray for my kids every morning, every night. I can't have a picture of their mother either. If you cry every day in here, you'll never survive.

At first I just wanted to make it to October. My kids love Halloween. Then I just wanted to make it to Christmas. And now, if it wasn't for the encouragement that I get when I talk to my kids, I couldn't make it to the end of the trial. Thank God, I can talk to them twice a week.

Then I hear from them: "How much longer, Dad?" I've got to be up when I'm talking to them. It hurts when I get off the phone with my kids. I break down every time I talk to them. Just the other day on the phone, my daughter Sydney, in a five-minute conversation, told me several times: "I love you, Daddy." I know she hears whatever she hears about me and she deals with it. I know this because I talk to her about the crazy things people are saying. I say to her and my son Justin: "I loved Mommy and Mommy loved all of us. Mommy's watching you and loves you." I told them I'm with the police and we're trying to find out what happened to Mommy. And I tell them most of all: "Daddy's safe."

My son says: "Why can't you come here and do it here, Daddy, why can't you come here?" A year ago on Father's Day, before all this happened, Justin gave me a little note on a small sheet of paper pasted on a large sheet that also contained impressions of his footprints.

Dear Dad,

Sometimes you get discouraged because I am so small and leave all my dirty marks on furniture and wall. But everyday I'm growing.... I'll be all grown someday and all those tiny dirty marks will finally fade away. Til then, plase save my footprint, so you can still recall, exactly what my feet were like when I was very small.

Love,

Justin
Happy Father's Day

The last time I was home, it was still hanging on my bathroom door.

I could never let my kids see me like this, in jail, with a chain around me, and chained to the floor. I could never let my kids see me like this. I'm their hero, and for them to even see me like this — the pain that's in this place.... Sometimes I just can't talk about it, even think about it.

To be unjustly accused of something, for people to try to convict you of something you didn't do and then to know if they succeed.... If that happens, if they succeed, I could never see my kids again. I will never let my kids come in here and see me — I will never let my kids come in and see me. I would rather have them feel that I was with their mother.

My kids don't deserve what is happening. I feel like they're also being punished. I've got to keep it together for my kids. I know in my heart I've been a good person. I'm not ashamed of my life. Of course I've done things in my life I would have changed. I look back on those things now and I feel some guilt. But someday Sydney and Justin will look me in the eye and know their father.

I've been told by their grandparents they haven't cried yet. They haven't shed any tears. They know their mother's in heaven now. They're only nine and six. The older they get, I think, the more they'll feel the pain. Sydney, I know, will express the pain when she sees me. I know that within ten days of us being back together, within ten days she will, one night, break into tears about her mommy. I know that, and I will sit there and hold her in my arms, no matter how old she is.

My Kids

This is Halloween 1986 and Sydney Brooke — yes, her middle name is Brooke, and she's just one year old. Nicole got the little costume and we both cut the pumpkin into a jack-o'-lantern. Each year the circle of kids who went trick-or-treating got larger.

*Here I am reading to Justin in the den of our home on Rocking-
ham Drive. We're going through this little picture book with a few
words. I'm leaning back on one of the quilts my mother made for
me. In the photograph on the left Justin is an infant and Sydney
has her collection of Barbie dolls.*

☙

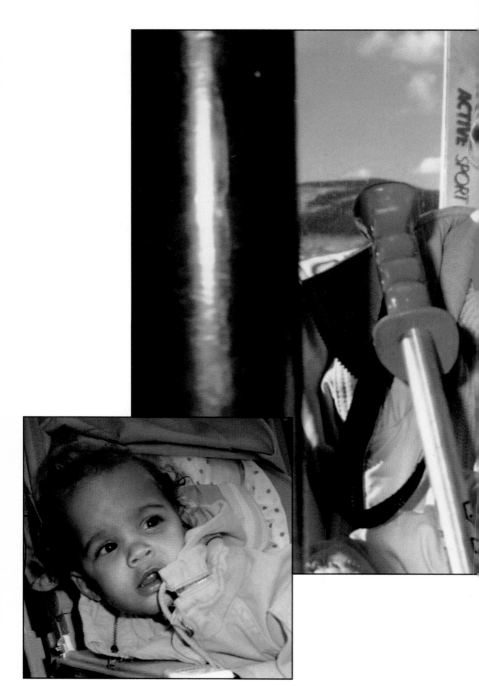

*Here we are again in Vail, Colorado, in a gondola going up the hill.
Before the kids could ski we used to strap them on our backs like a
papoose and Nicole and I would ski down with them. On the left
Sydney is in her stroller in Brentwood.*

❧

I'm so proud of Arnelle. She's the first Simpson in our family to graduate from college. Here we are at Howard University. The reason I say the "first Simpson" is because I didn't finish USC. Things just got too busy. The picture on the right was taken at the time that Jason graduated from the Army and Navy Academy in Carlsbad, California. He's a great cook like my dad and is now an assistant chef. I'm so proud of both of these kids.

Here is Sydney in one of Nicole's outfits. Those hands that you can hardly see behind Sydney are Nicole's, holding our daughter up for the picture. Sydney was just under a year old. She kind of looks like Lana Turner here.

Part 2

The Working Press

Dear Mr. Simpson,

I never thought I would agree with Associate Justice Clarence Thomas on any issue, but his "high-tech lynching" definitely applies to what is happening to you and I would like to know how the Press, Law Enforcement, and the Judicial system plan to give you and your family your life back.

The Grace of our Lord and Savior Jesus Christ protect you always.

Ashley Craig
New York, NY

Dear O.J.,

Are you still hanging in there?
I was watching something interesting earlier today on C-SPAN II. It was "O.J. and the Media." It's

amazing how little the media knows about this Country
and our Constitution. Most wouldn't recognize the
Fourth Amendment if it hit them in the face.

Love and Prayers,

Mrs. Ray L. Newton
Louisville, IL

What hurt me on that Monday after I returned to L.A. from Chicago, adding to the death of Nicole, was the press and how they behaved. The first week almost killed me. Along with the grief I was having over Nicole's murder, I literally felt I was murdered. I felt there were three homicides. Some unknown killers murdered Nicole and Ronald Goldman; now the press was murdering me. They were tired of Loni and Burt, I guess. It's a sad commentary on the press, isn't it?

From the very first, the press wanted to believe my guilt, that I was guilty of these murders. I could understand how easy it was for people to believe that I did this, but I realized that it wasn't the people who started believing that I was guilty, it was the press. My ex-wife is dead; Nicole is buried. Once she is buried, there's no more story. But if I can appear to be guilty, it's a great story, and it starts to make money for everybody.

What I became aware of quickly was that the press doesn't care about the truth, they only care about what sells. If two or three other guys showed up tomorrow — I mean, were arrested for these murders — forget it. White, black, half white, quarter black, maybe it would be headlines for a day or a week. Then in a month it's forgotten. But as long as O.J. is the suspect, this story is money. It's ratings, and ratings mean money. They wouldn't be doing this story if it wasn't for money.

I knew the press wasn't the hardest-working class in this country, but I never thought they were this lazy. The lazy reporting, the false reports... They never investigated the information they were receiving, whether it was truthful or not. What the press basically did was wait for the next leak or the next rumor. Now that I have the right to look at videotapes connected with my case, I look at the coverage in those first days and weeks and I can't believe all the reporters just sitting around. The press just sat around outside my house and Nicole's house and waited for the next leak.

———————

Dear O.J.,

To an innocent man that the media has convicted before the courts have had a chance to view the case. I always thought this was the land of the free, home of the brave.

The media is blowing your case all out of proportion. All the coverage isn't necessary. The media acted like a pack of hungry dogs after one dog bone. They should be ashamed of themselves.

The media also talks like you're a trophy. You're a living, breathing MAN with feelings like everybody else. CLEAR YOUR MIND AND STAY FOCUSED.

Much Love!

Your buddy, Andrea Smith
Fresno, CA

P.S. Even if you never receive this letter I feel better because I wrote it!

————————

There are members of the media whom I respected in the past and it hurts me to find that they are part of this lazy reporting. Dan Rather hurt me. I always thought of him as Walter Cronkite or Edward R. Murrow. He was a frontline guy to me, a man with some personal integrity, like a David Brinkley. But his reporting was almost the last straw. It was a time when I was wanting to join Nicole. Al Cowlings had gotten out of his white Bronco and I remember I was alone in the car. Dan Rather was on the radio and he started talking about eight or nine different reports of domestic spousal abuse calls from my house and I had to say to myself: Where in the hell does that number nine come from? With all the pain in me, it was just another spear. I can say it was devastating. You expect with this guy to get the truth. Now I say to Dan Rather: "Just do a little research and you'll find out the truth." At first Barbara Walters had it all wrong, about my alimony payments as a possible motive. She said I had high payments and that my income was down. When in fact it was just the opposite. I was making more money than I ever had made before and I had no alimony payments to Nicole. I had made a cash settlement with Nicole at the time of our divorce. Barbara Walters has kind of made amends on the air because she admitted that her facts were wrong. And to think that Connie Chung would contribute to the promotion of Faye Resnick's tabloid book. Why would Connie Chung have her on her show? I'm sure the answer is ratings.

That's what TV is all about. Ratings. The court, the prosecution, and my defense are going to make all these experts explain their credentials. Those who will testify as expert witnesses will have to justify whatever they have to say. Don't you think the press should use a little of the same procedure? Shouldn't the press be spelling out the credentials of the sources they talk to? Shouldn't the public know the credentials of those people providing leaks to the media?

At one point, my family was so outraged at what was being said by so many people in the media. I didn't want to fight it out in the press, I didn't want a public debate. I wanted to save everything for testimony in court where it would really count. And my lawyers were telling me it would be inappropriate for me to talk to the press. But the jury pool was being poisoned. The press was out of control. Everybody started interpreting my relationship with Nicole to fit their own — or someone's — view of my personal life. They were accusing me of about every bad thing you could think of. I felt I didn't want to be dragging my family and friends through the mud of whatever was going on. But my family was really outraged; my mother was mad; so many of my friends were outraged. My older children, my sister Shirley, my mother needed to speak out for their own sakes, not for me. They wanted the world to know that I was not capable of committing this crime. At the end I said okay. I am blessed with a wonderful family.

Dear Mr. Simpson:

To be honest, I don't know if you are innocent or guilty. I simply believe you are innocent until proven guilty.

I want to tell you, contrary to what the media would have you believe, most of America has not decided you are guilty. I think most people are willing to let the court decide. I personally believe the media has been very biased, they give the prosecution more air time, etc.... I don't believe anyone can make a judgment based on press releases when they don't give both sides.

I truly believe most of America feels this way.

We hope you feel the moral support from all across the country!

Sincerely,

Jennifer Czawlytko & family
Baltimore, MD

Dear Mr. Simpson,

I read that article in Newsweek *where they criticized you for living white, and never looking back at where you came from.*

The whole article pissed me off. The whole thing had a bad smell to it; and finally I realized what all this hoopla was about concerning you; and it all boiled down to racism. Because you are famous and have money, the white world accepted you; but underneath, the white men were seething; that you dared to marry their women....

Sincerely,

Roy Lott
Richmond, CA

Newsweek did a story on me the third or fourth week after my arrest, entitled "The Double Life of O.J. Simpson," that wasn't lazy reporting. No, it was worse: it was pure racism. By the way I read it, they used me as an example of blacks lusting after a white world. It was racist in its tone and feel. It was the most false, racist article I've ever read. For example, they published a picture on the first page of the story that really pissed me off. It showed a redheaded stripper, with me watching her in some seamy position. She's white, I'm black. The kind of shot you might think was taken in some sleazy bar. The caption in big white letters was blatantly misleading: "Duty and Obsession. He was a perfectionist who doggedly worked to fit into the white world — affable, genial and unthreatening. But Nicole left him. And his black friends scorned him for lusting after only white women." That caption was all wrong. Now I know that the old cliché "One picture speaks louder than a thousand words" is true. First: I would like to know which black friends of mine, that I have hung out with over the years, scorned me. *Newsweek* never gave one single name. Second: The facts behind this picture are simply these: The picture was taken in 1989 in the back yard of my home, with my in-laws, my kids, Nicole, and some 350 of our friends present. It was my birthday and it was Arnelle's graduation from high school. So we just rolled all these events into one big party. Somebody sent this comic stripper to the party as a joke, as a fun present for my birthday. But now the picture comes out in *Newsweek* cropped so that it looks like it's just her right in front of me in some sleazy hangout. The photographer who took that picture knows the truth and *Newsweek* had a responsibility to report the truth, where and when that photo was taken.

In another photograph in *Newsweek,* they showed a picture of me with four young contestants at the Miss "Hawaiian Tropic" suntan promotion that I was a guest at. *Newsweek* again gave a false impression about the photograph. They placed a caption on the picture that read: "PARTY GUY: The pitchman was also a high liver who, sources said, took drugs and joined in random sex." What has this got to do with that photograph? What *Newsweek* was doing was making an editorial comment and using a photograph to support their preconceived idea of my lifestyle. *Newsweek* criticized me for choosing a predominantly white school when I enrolled in USC. They gave the impression that if you are black you are not supposed to go to a place like USC. What they forgot to tell their readers was that in 1916 the first All American from USC was in fact black and his name was Bryce Taylor. They forgot that people like Charles White, Marcus Allen, Anthony Davis, Ricky Bell, Lynn Swann, and myself went to USC because of the school's great athletic heritage and not because of the color of the skin of people who were at the university.

The problem is that the press wants to deal only with the sensational aspects of this story. Now, at least Larry King televised a fair debate about this article. He had a black civil rights lawyer going up against the writer of the *Newsweek* article. They discussed if this article was, in fact, racist, and whether it was fair to me. That was good journalism.

Time magazine's first coverage of my arrest showed my arrest photo on the cover. But they retouched it, darkened it — it was pure racism! The photo on *Time*'s cover also spoke a thousand words, a thousand words with a twisted meaning. Racist stereotyping. But *Time* magazine was responsible enough to publicly state that they had made a mistake in altering the photograph. Will *Newsweek* ever reprint that picture of me and the stripper with a corrected, truthful caption?

Dear O.J.,

This country we live in is supposed to be the best in the world, the land of opportunity. You are living proof of that! Why then do we build heroes, just to tear them down at the first chance we get?

The media are the worst offenders. They are robbing you of your "presumption of innocence."

God Bless You, and I know He will.

Sincerely,

Jane Gentile
Hasbrouck Heights, NJ

What has hurt me the most is that in covering this story, the legitimate press became the "tabloid press." In that first month, in those first weeks, it seemed as if the legitimate press didn't check any of their stories. The legitimate press used what the tabloid press was saying as their source of information. It became a race to see who had the latest leak, the latest news, and they didn't care if it was true or false. It went far beyond exaggeration. It was even beyond irresponsibility. It was a rat race, it just became a frenzy: Let's get a new story, we don't care if it's true or false.

I always knew that the press could be like leeches. I'm not the only celebrity to get mauled like this. Look at Michael Jackson and the charges against him, just look how they jumped on Burt Reynold's financial problems. We all know the press thrives on the negative. That's what the public wants and that's what the public gets — the negative. But I also always thought there was some point in time where you can deal with — where you can control, at least to some extent — the press's exaggeration. Now I don't know if anyone really can.

Dear Mr. Simpson:

I have written letters to a number of news reporters here in Texas who have offered their editorials about you, and it really pisses me off, royally! The biggest issue that I have, other than the lies, is when this is all over will these jerks and witches who report this crap spend as much time apologizing to you, your friends, your family, and to me? Will they all put on the front pages of their newspapers, magazines, and live television broadcasts how wrong they all were, how unfair they all were and how their behavior did nothing to serve the public, our justice system or the privacy and reputation of a man, a human being?

*My answer is NO! They certainly won't and what
little any of them could offer would not be of any genuine
value.*

Thank you for the time, O.J.

Take Care,

*Terri J. Watson
Kansas City, MO*

I get all my current news by telephone. But there's a TV here
in jail that I can watch. It's rolled up to my cell on a cart, just
on the other side of the bars. I don't have a remote, so I have to
live with the channel that the deputies set. One night I was
watching *Hard Copy*, not that I like the show, but it happened
to be on the channel the TV was set on that night. They had
this 240-pound woman talking about me, a piano player who
worked in a cocktail lounge. The big scoop of the day! Here
she's talking about how some twenty-five years ago, when I was
playing for the Bills and was there for an exhibition game
against the Jets, I somehow got her up against the wall, trying
to make out with her. It really had me cracking up. They
showed a picture of her twenty-five years ago and she looked as
big as she looks now. Then they had a member of her band,
some drummer, who supposedly saw the whole thing. Now all
this is supposed to have happened in George Wallace's

Alabama. You think I tried to assault a white woman twenty-five years ago in George Wallace's state? Give me a break!! I just had to stop looking. I could not change channels.

I used to debate with myself about writing to the *National Enquirer* whenever they wrote something false or misleading about me or Nicole. That was before this tragedy. I always said to myself then: Leave it alone. Now I'm of the opinion that you can't let things alone. It's like a cancer; it just keeps on growing.

One of the tabloids did a beautiful story on Paula, a very complimentary story, quoting Paula. Paula didn't say half the things they printed, at any time. So if I'm not going to accept the negative lies, then I can't accept the positive lies. Truth is truth, good or bad. Now these distorted stories will never be erased from the minds of the public. That is why I don't believe in public opinion polls. What does the public get to base their opinions on?

Dear O.J.,

> *I have explained to my children (ages 9 & 10) not to believe everything they see or hear on the news, and that we all know more about your case than we should know because of misconduct on the part of the L.A. County Attorney and the L.A. Police Department (I have also*

written to them stating as much).

O.J., you are loved, in the best sense of the word.

Sincerely,

Edward Neal, Jr.
Cokato, MN

Of course, every once in a while the press does something really good. The Larry King show I mentioned before or the early days of Watergate. Now this young lady, Susan Smith, who murdered her two children in South Carolina. All along, she was so convincing. She told police some black gunman stole her car and drove away with her kids. She gave the description of a black man and even helped in drawing his picture. She was on every TV show, morning and night. Then some type of anger started to build up. The press started really looking closely at her story and all the facts. Here the public was starting to get angry and that anger was starting to be directed against this unknown black man, but the local press didn't buy into that.

What the public was missing in their anger was whether anyone could pull off a crime like that one in South Carolina. Could a black man go anywhere with two little white babies and not be noticed? The press down there didn't miss that. The press kept the pressure on. This woman eventually could not live with herself. Eventually she had to tell someone. I think a person like that can be convincing for a day or a week. But as the enormity of what had been done dawned on her, if she had any kind of goodness, any kind of religion in her, the enormity of what she did eventually forced her to confess under the pressure of the police and the press.

Everybody is talking about Mrs. Smith. Like I said before, it's the guilty person, the criminal, or the person that the press makes out to be guilty who draws media attention. That's the story that'll get the ratings. For instance, nobody is really talking much about something that happened in California in November of 1994. To me it's more interesting than the tragedy in South Carolina, but it's getting very little coverage. Here in Bakersfield, there is a guy named Tomlin getting out of jail after sixteen years. He was framed for a murder and convicted. The key witness came forward and recanted her story and admitted she lied. It still takes another eight years to get this guy out of jail. This black guy spent sixteen years of his life in jail, totally framed by the police. Apparently everything at the time of his trial pointed to his guilt, not his innocence. I look at him and I look at myself.

The prosecution, the press, can take just about everything I've done in the last five years of my life, and somehow make it look like all of it was leading up to murder. The thing is we could take almost anybody's life and do the same thing. If we're going to look at everything assuming guilt up front, and say, "This is an indication…and that…and now look at what happened on this date." You pick and choose facts. That's all someone needs to make a case.

Sometimes I get the press and the prosecution mixed up. Who is who? One day the press is fitting the facts to justify its conclusion. The prosecution is doing the same thing, finding only the facts that justify its conclusion of "guilty."

Hi, O.J.,

They say you are the news of the decade. I can believe that, but they never tell any of your good points. It's always "damaging evidence," as they put it. I guess this is another reason God didn't make me a "somebody." I'd probably be in jail for assaulting the press.

Love to you,

Lucy Richardson
Macon, MO

It looks like in everything I'm ever going to do for the rest of my life, I will have to consider what the press is going to make out of it. I'll be found innocent, but the press will never leave me alone if it will sell another paper. When we were making funeral arrangements, like the viewing of Nicole's body, I wanted to have a private viewing the day before the funeral. Nicole's family had been thinking of opening it up to the public but I wouldn't let that happen. I knew the press. I knew their zeal, their new fancy hidden cameras; I knew that unless the viewing was private, my kids and I would be seeing it in magazines, in the rags, and on TV— we'd be seeing Nicole in her casket.

Justice and Injustice

Dear O.J.,

    Hang in there!
    Please believe that there are people in America who still believe anyone is innocent until proven guilty.

                God bless you!

                Earl & Pat Brown & Family
                Waynesville, NC

Dear O.J.,

    The law protects criminals rather than victims. The criminals enjoy the benefits of law and victims suffer the consequences.

Criminals with money either are punished less or get away with it.

A hopeful and law-abiding Citizen of the United States. Brooklyn, NY

I don't believe in the legal system anymore. I do believe in people, individual people within any system. Right now I have to get twelve people to listen to all the facts, to listen to me, and for the first time in my life that's not going to be easy.

Our justice system has gotten to the point where all that matters is winning. Winning at all costs. Winning at all costs is the reason I don't believe in the system anymore.

This game aspect has gotten to the point where the prosecution can go to Arizona, as they did, and present their case against me to a mock jury. They're trying to find out which citizens are better suited for the prosecution. I mean, better suited for a conviction. Now I find myself in a place where I even have to have my own expert, an expert on jurors to tell me which citizens are going to be more suited for me. When you're doing that kind of "scientific" research, you're not after justice anymore, you're after winning. My own lawyers are part of the system.

What I want is the truth to come out and I want justice. And the only people left I can believe in to provide justice are the jurors. I have faith that real people, regular people, will be able to see the truth.

Dear Mr. Simpson,

My name is Terrienna Willie, and I admire the way you have upheld yourself, especially your integrity.

I dream to rise in a society that sees me as "just another black child." See, you were a superstar, now the media "wants" us to see you as just another blackman accused of killing two members of the Anglo-Saxon race.

Sincerely,

Terrienna Willie
Desoto, TX

I never used to notice how many people in a room were black or white. But now I have been placed in a position where I sit in the courtroom and I count how many blacks just walked in, how many Asians, how many Hispanics, how many whites. The system has forced me to look at the jury from a racial point of view. Now I ask myself: Who lives in downtown L.A.? Who lives in Orange County?

Can there be any real justice in this type of thinking? I have never thought this way before and I don't like it.

I came from one of the most racially diverse communities in America, San Francisco. I came from a hodge-podge, a cornucopia of races. My mother was truly color-blind. In the projects we were all colors, and all kind of poor. She treated each person on his merits and taught us to do the same. I never in my life looked at race.

Somehow the system has polarized society on this whole racial issue. I thought we had a big breakthrough in the sixties and all of a sudden it looks like we're regressing again. I have lived my entire life based on merit, where you are judged on your ability, how well you do something, not on the color of your skin. I played ball because I was good, not because I was black. Now I'm on the inside of the legal system and not outside of it. Maybe I was naive in the past, but now I've been forced to become aware that so much of this case is racial. Skin color shouldn't matter. Justice should be blind. But when the first twelve members of the jury were picked, I knew the TV news that night and the newspapers the next morning would all focus on the racial makeup of the jury. I believe strongly that that is wrong.

It's interesting that so many of the questions to the jury pool had to do with an image of O.J. as a good guy. It is curious, and it's difficult for me, to sit there and hear the prosecution try to put into these prospective jurors' minds that if you went around with a camera, and edited all the times someone saw me smiling, it wouldn't be a true image of me. They are trying to say that the O.J. you see on TV isn't the O.J. that's away from the camera. Well, see, I strongly disagree with the prosecution. And I'm saying that's a road that they can't survive going down.

If they talk to people, no matter what they may think about my guilt or innocence, if the prosecution talks to people who know me, who've been around me, then they have to know that I'm the same guy on and off the screen. I don't play O.J. when I'm on TV. I'm always me.

Dear Mr. Simpson,

I really wish there was a way I could be selected to the jury. I would make sure you didn't get railroaded. But there's little chance of that. I'm just a few hundred miles north of your district.

Tell Mr. Cowlings how very grateful we are to him for keeping you alive that frightening day in the Bronco.

God Bless You.

Mrs. Sheril Luke
Porterville, CA

I've been looking every day at the panel of prospective jurors. I look at these people and ask myself: Why do they want to be on this jury? And I say to myself that everybody wants to be part of something. When the circus comes to town, everybody wants to get a glimpse when the circus parade comes down the road. Everybody slows down and takes a look when there's a car accident. And my trial has become the biggest circus in the country. One day I may see three or four prospective jurors that I feel would never convict me in a million years no matter what the evidence was. Then I see five or six prospective jurors that, no matter what the evidence is, are going to convict me. I don't want either group on the jury. I want people who will listen carefully and decide on the facts. If they decide on the facts in court, I'm not worried.

Dear Mr. Simpson,

Just because everything is pointing to you doesn't mean you're guilty. Well, I used to think that people with money have it made. Now I really see for myself that money doesn't really mean anything.

You have problems just like everybody else. I must admit I wouldn't want to be in your shoes for anything in the world.

O.J., we really do care.

Mary Myers
Racine, WI

I hired two lawyers. I hired Robert Shapiro and I hired Johnnie Cochran. Then they brought all the other attorneys and consultants into my case. Would you believe over fifteen people? Then Skip Taft, my personal attorney, came to me and started talking about the cost of everything — millions of dollars. I said to him: "The cost of my life? If this is what it takes, if this is what it's going to take, then go take it." If I had cancer, I'd spend it all. Or if Sydney had cancer, or Justin. If Nicole's mother, Judy Brown, if my mother, if anybody I loved were sick, if it took every dime I had, every dime I had saved, I would spend it. What the hell, it's not something you even have to think about.

Then I say to myself: If I didn't have some money, I would have no chance at all. I wouldn't be able to afford all these people who will help in getting me out of here. I truly realize now, for the first time, that there are probably a great many people in jail who are innocent, but who don't have the money to prove it in court. It's a higher percentage than anybody would think. In the past, I didn't pay attention to those types of stories. But now I do. Seeing how the police handled my case has made me more aware. If they want to get you, they're going to get you.

———

Simply - you are guilty.
Simply - you are not a man.
Simply - assume responsibility for your actions.

An innocent man would have offered all his hairs for
analysis - you held back because
you are guilty.

> *[Unsigned]*
> *Postmark: Brooklyn, NY*

c/o Mr. O.J. Simpson
Dear Mr. Johnnie Cochran,

*You seem to attack DNA evidence at every turn —
how then is it that some people who have spent 15 years
in jail are being let out now because DNA testing, even
after all these years, has proved their innocence? If O.J. is
innocent, he should be delighted to have blood and hair
tested — it wouldn't be his if he had not been at the murder scene. I am beginning to detest defense attorneys,
since they are not in the least interested in truth
or justice.*

Regards,

Mrs. Carmie R. Richesin
Telluride, CO

A lot of the evidence is going to be DNA. There's going to be a lot on both sides. What's funny about this is that I have read about this DNA stuff. I read mystery books all the time. My favorite writer is Clive Cussler. I like Jeffrey Archer and Ken Follett. I used to like Ludlum but I can't read him anymore. It's all the same kind of predictable. I love Nelson DeMille and Patricia Cornwell, who was a coroner, sort of morbid. Her character is a coroner in Richmond, Virginia, named Dr. Kay Scarpetta. I've read most of her books. I'm an avid reader of English detective novels. Great stuff.

I know DNA* is going to have a lot to do with my life during this trial. But, unlike in books of fiction, I've been told that there are real scientific problems connected to DNA. The prosecution is trying to use DNA to convict me, but I'm innocent.

Dear O.J.,

In my personal opinion, the Prosecuting Attorney Marcia Clark will do everything in her power to have you found guilty, because you are a black man.

I believe the prosecutors will go to any length to find people who will back them.

Of course, I know the prosecutors must go to any length to win this case because they have lost so many high-profile cases, such as the Menendez trial and the Rodney King beating.

You are in my thoughts and prayers.

Sincerely,

Mary L. David
Maplewood, MN

---

*DNA. A nucleic acid that carries the genetic information in the cell and is capable of self-replication and synthesis of RNA. DNA consists of two long chains of nucleotides twisted into a double helix and joined by hydrogen bonds between the complementary bases adenine and thymine or cytosine and guanine. The sequence of nucleotides determines individual hereditary characteristics. Source: *American Heritage Dictionary*

I do have one major problem with my case. I can't vary my story to fit a scenario. I can only tell the truth. The prosecution can go down a certain road and when it doesn't work, they can go down another road, and when that doesn't work they can go down a third road. Already the prosecution has two different versions of what happened the night Nicole was killed. They'll keep going down roads till they find the most plausible scenario for them to win the case. They've gone down so many different roads they couldn't have believed in all of them. But there is only one road I can go down. That's the road of telling the truth. I did not commit these murders.

Philosophically, I can sit back and watch what the prosecution is doing. I understand their role. But I also have the knowledge of when they mislead and exaggerate. As much as I may hear the prosecution talk about a fair trial and all that, they're not after justice — they're after me.

Dear O.J.,

It was very obvious to me that the police concocted their "emergency" story, rehearsed before climbing over the wall.

Do me a favor, please use my attached check to help protect my 4th Amendment rights and your case.

Sincerely, a concerned citizen.

Arthur Burton
Campbell, CA

Dear O.J. Simpson:

I'm 75 yrs old, fought in World War II. I was shot four times to uphold the Constitution and the Fourth Amendment. Most of my buddies are on top of Omaha Beach, white crosses as far as you can see.

I'm a white man but it always seems a black man doesn't have a chance.

California is making a mockery of the Fourth Amendment.

Your true friend,

Russell Dottery
Scottsdale, AZ

I don't think any amendment to the Constitution should take precedence over any other amendment. Should freedom of speech be more important than somebody's right to a fair trial? If I look back at Detectives Fuhrman and Vannatter, who entered my property without a search warrant, I can see what the system has done to my Fourth Amendment* rights. That's

---

*The Fourth Amendment: The right of the people to be secure in their persons, houses, papers, and effects, against unreasonable searches and seizures, shall not be violated, and no warrants shall issue, but upon probable cause, supported by oath or affirmation and particularly describing the place to be searched, and the persons or things to be seized.

the one that's supposed to protect all of us from "unreasonable search and seizure." The public is looking at me as a mirror of what could happen to them.

No single individual, whatever position he might have, whatever his suspicions might be, should be above the law. And, in my opinion, what the LAPD did when they went over the wall — these police detectives without a search warrant—was to violate my constitutional rights.

Dear O.J. Simpson,

I know the jury will find you innocent. The truth is that you're a wonderful, gorgeous man who has done nothing wrong at all ever. I know you really loved Nicole Brown and would never, ever do anything to hurt her.

All my Love Always,

Colette Peschel
Woodbridge, CT

Dear O.J.

You are the most handsomest black man I have ever seen.

Love ya always and forever.

Gay Ezette Priester
Houston, TX

Sometimes I think my physical presence does play a part in my case. Having these TV cameras in the court all the time is a no-win situation for me. If I'm looking like I'm having a good day in court, if I'm too jovial, people say he's not serious or concerned enough. If I'm looking worried or upset, then it looks like I did it. You just can't win. I think the worst thing the court can do is let the TV camera in. I disagreed with my lawyers on that, I disagreed with everybody around me on the issue of allowing a TV camera in the courtroom. I think by allowing TV coverage in the courtroom, you're going to infringe on so many people's personal lives. Some of the people being brought to the witness stand on both sides during the trial will have to talk about some very personal things. Friends of mine are going to be asked a lot of very personal questions about their lives and my life. It's enough to let the press write about their take on it. Reading about it isn't the same as seeing it on TV and it doesn't affect the people who have to testify in the same way. I even feel bad for the coroner, Irwin Golden, who was on the stand before the eyes of the country. This guy can't go anywhere right now without everyone looking at him. He's now recognized everywhere he goes, even ostracized for one reason or another.

Dear Mr. Simpson:

Since you have chosen to face the world and stand as tall as ever, I pray that you draw comfort from the strength

above and from those who love and cherish you dearly.
You are not alone in your sadness and misery; you are only
by yourself in your surroundings. I care dearly.

God's Peace & Love,

Evelyn Joyce Hightower
Youngstown, OH

My biggest concern is what all of this has done to me inside. I never really felt hatred before. But now I have, for the first time in my life. This bothers me. Two things seem to be coming at me at once. One is race, because when you get into this system race becomes an issue. An overwhelming issue. The second is the false impression of who I am. The prosecution has an agenda to try to tear down who I am, to imply I'm someone other than the person I have been all these years.

Dear O.J.

Be strong and do not let that prosecutor intimidate you — she is only doing a job.

Again, may God be with you.

Marlene Laporte
Brooklyn, NY

I'm going to come out of this with my dignity intact. I've been saying from the very beginning: Let me get in front of the jury. Let everybody say what they're going to say, then I'll get up there and say my piece — and let them judge. That's what I've done throughout my life. Judge me for what I've done, for what I'm showing you. Judge me for my actions. In the end, I'll have my dignity intact.

Spousal Abuse

Mr. Simpson,

One thing I wanted to say, everyone is focusing on the alleged abuse you inflicted on your ex-wife. No one has mentioned the abuse she inflicted on you. In the tapes that were aired this past week, it stated that you were extremely violent towards her sometime last year. What I heard in the tapes, was someone who exercised incredible control when up against this situation. Based on what was said in the tapes, I commend you for striking out at something else and not at her. I understand some of the torture you endured over the years. The difference between physical abuse and emotional abuse is one you can see with your eyes. Emotional abuse is much more difficult, but even more damaging.

I was a victim of emotional abuse by my paramour. We were together for thirteen years. I can understand the anger, frustration, jealousy, insecurities, low self-esteem you might have felt in dealing with your ex.

If you are guilty of this crime, it would be very sad. But I understand. There are people out there, men and women, who enjoy playing games, who enjoy hurting.

No one knows how they would react to loving some-one to such an extent, making sacrifices, and in return suffering humiliation and degradation.

Keep the faith, guilty or not. HOLD YOUR HEAD UP. EUNICE SIMPSON worked hard raising her baby boy and I am sure you have made her PROUD. GOD BE WITH YOU ALWAYS.

> *J. Miller*
> *Jamaica, NY*

Dear O.J.,

When I was married my husband and I had a very similar relationship. I said a lot of the same things to the police as Nicole did. But what I didn't confess, and I believe is the same in your situation, is that I was as much to blame for the disturbance. Calling the police was more my way of gaining control.

> *Always in my thoughts,*

> *Tracie Bechke*
> *Cleveland, OH*

Mr. Simpson:

While I lived in fear for my life on several occasions, I am living proof that domestic violence does not always culminate in murder. Spousal abuse is a horrible thing, and I hope those acts of violence were not witnessed by your children. Those lovely children have lost their mother, and they will grieve for her for an eternity. How would they cope with the fact that their father murdered her? I want you to be innocent of these crimes — innocent for the sake of your children. BUT if the evidence presented at trial links you positively, without any doubt, to the murders, then you must suffer the consequences.

I hope you are encouraged to know that there are people who can be fair and make decisions based on facts alone.

Sincerely,

Donna K. Brown
Bowling Green, KY

Dear O.J.,

We are taught from childhood by our Mom and Dad to respect the female from our Mom and Dad. We find ourselves so lost as a man when it's us that's being abused. So we carry it within us day after day, in hope that tomorrow things will be better. For your deep love for her never changed.

With society as it is, there's no place we can run to without being ashamed. We were raised this way from day one.

There are no abused husband shelters that a man can run to. In each town there are shelters for children or wives who are abused.

Let the world know the male finds nowhere he can turn.

Sincerely,

D. E. B.
Satanta, KS

Hi, O.J.,

I don't appreciate those sneaky bastards releasing those 911* audiotapes. I think it was deliberately on their behalf.

A fan forever,

Steve Dick
Latham, NY

---

*911: Shortly after the arrest of O.J., the police department of Los Angeles released, to the press, audio copies of two 911 calls made by Nicole Brown Simpson. One call was placed on New Year's Eve 1989 and the other was placed on October 25, 1993.

Dear O.J. Simpson,

If the woman be black or white there's no need for abuse. Oh sure, we all know through a marriage or relationship there are misunderstandings. Sometimes we do not agree with ourselves, so, agreeing with others is a problem. But abuse? Come on.

Concerned Sister,

Lynette Clay
Chicago, IL

Dear Mr. Simpson:

I don't condone domestic violence as I, too, was involved in a similar situation 10 years ago and hightailed it out of there with my son. I do believe, however, that after the first incident, you didn't hit your wife again. Instead, you took it out on the walls, the doors, the furniture, etc. We all have fits of temper and the anger is worse when the ones we love "push those buttons." We've all pushed someone else's buttons at one point or another in our lives to see what type of reaction we would get or did so willingly because we knew what the reaction would be and then use the same reaction against the individual in one form or another. A simple case of the end justifying the means or, as familiarly termed, manipulation.

Ella Wheeler Wilcox, an American poet, once said, "The only folks who give us pain are those we love the best." In my opinion, truer words were never spoken.

Sincerely,

JoAnne Kolocotrones Newby
Cape Coral, FL

Dear O.J.,

I can't believe that your ex-wife was afraid of you. You don't have dinner with or live down the street from someone that you think is going to kill you.

If someone is afraid of someone else, then they do their best to go away. There is always a way for the father to see the children.

Also, as a lady, I know that we can mentally abuse men if we know that they care a lot for us. Well, I think men can too. But mental abuse can be more abusive than physical.

Love and friendship

Barbara Johnson
Fresno, CA

O.J.—

I was a victim of Domestic Violence. My husband fit your profile—handsome, charismatic, all the women

just thought he was wonderful — co-workers and friends
of both sexes thought he could do no wrong. The
reality is, he deceived them all. I lived with him for
nearly 18 years and am lucky I am alive today.

What I am telling you is, I feel confident you are
guilty — you could never fool me — and I hope the jury
can see through you.

[Unsigned]
Postmark: Milpitas, CA

Spousal abuse will be an issue at my trial and therefore I can't discuss it in these pages. I would however like to say that the spousal abuse groups that are advocating tougher laws, better education, and other things that are important to society — I agree with these points of view. The public needs to be awakened to the issue. But when a celebrity is involved it becomes newsworthy. It becomes hot.

What I don't agree with is that in using my case, these groups don't care about the facts of my case. The truth to them doesn't matter. These groups don't really care about Nicole. The truth of my case doesn't matter as long as it helps promote what they're trying to do. They want to use my situation as some type of an endorsement for why their cause is just. They don't care if what they are saying is true or false. They only care that my name is O.J. Simpson. That works for them, that gets them more publicity.

I don't believe any good can come out of deceit and I'm suspicious of any person or organization that's willing to use deceit to gain any kind of good.

Dear O.J.,

   Your awful ordeal has already had some positive aspects. There is increased awareness of the seriousness of battery of women. There is the recognition that the battering man is also a victim.
   I believe that we are often used to further causes which we do not choose or understand. You have years ahead of you to do good. Where this work happens and how are not known to anyone now but you have a unique opportunity because you are O.J. and are greatly loved.

                  Sincerely,

                  Maxine Erkiletian
                  Rolla, MO

I hope that by the end of the legal process I'm involved in, America will open its eyes to many issues, issues of the media, issues of the Constitution, issues that no longer should be taken for granted.

Racism

Dear O.J.:

I hope you are innocent because we live in a racist society where black men are condemned and tried before the case ever comes to trial.

Sincerely,

DeArmond J. Carter
Vienna, VA

Aah lookey here Sambo, it Done looks as if you is done jumping into bed with any more white women. Glory be and amen.

Now if something like this would only happen more often to Hollywood n—rs like say Quincy Jones or Mr. Poitier, the world would be a better place. Aint nothin worse than celebrity n—rs with money. The real problem you guys create is that you have a habit of leaving behind your genetic traces in the form of mullato muts. There should be a law passed to sterilize black males when they reach a certain income level. Lets face it, if you guys didn't have the bucks aint no white woman would go near you. I mean what woman wants to have sex with a primitive jungle man?

Good-by Juice, another coon in the can.

Karl K. King Jacksonville, FL

I've always known about racism. It's when any race feels superior over another race.

Now I get some letters that are pure racist. Some of them are signed, but many of them are not.

Two years ago if somebody wrote me a racist letter, my assistant, Cathy, would not have even shown it to me. I dealt with the issue by ignoring it. When I read the hate mail now, I say to myself: This person's got a problem and I can't solve it. I can't help this person. But when I read one of these letters, it stays with me all night. In the past I said: "These people have accepted things that aren't true, and they don't see they're not true. Maybe one day they'll see the light, but it's not my problem." I wouldn't give credence to anyone who wrote the big "N" word and all that stuff. Once in a while, I would be driving somewhere and some guy would drive up beside me and shout the "N" word. I would ignore it. I ignored racism. Since I was a kid I've avoided negatives. I always insulated myself from the subject of skin color.

Now I can't insulate myself from racism. It's everywhere I look. Now I read these racist letters and I don't want to ignore the issue anymore. When I get out of here, there'll be a lot I'll say on this issue.

Dear O.J.,

I remember you when you came to Birmingham to play Alabama at Legion Field here. And hey I don't know if you know it, but you and S.C. changed football here in the South. It made Bear Bryant realize that he couldn't keep on going on beating up on teams without the black players. It was hard for a lot of Alabama people to take but you, O.J. Simpson, changed that so football was never the same around here, and also thanks, O.J.

Hang in there, Bro.

Fred Young
Birmingham, AL

Thanks for the compliment, but I wasn't on that team. That was after I played for USC and they had Anthony Davis and Sam Cunningham. What a great team.

Twenty years ago I was on the top of the world. I was interested in making it, in succeeding. In 1975, I went to South Africa to a make a movie called *Diamond Mercenaries*. It was a long trip from New York, and Peter Fonda, who was also in the film, met me at the airport. He was all for causes and he promptly took me into a "white only" restroom at the airport. It was strange walking into this toilet with a cutout of a black figure above the door with a red line through it. It was like being in the South in the fifties.

Back then racism to me was a black-white thing. But in South Africa, I discovered racism was not limited to whites and blacks. And it was not just the racism of the Afrikaners I was exposed to.

One night, at Walvisbaai, I was invited for dinner at the home of a "colored" family. One of the sons was working on the film. This family was a working-class black family. They worked in the home of a white family as household staff. Looking at their skin color, it wasn't much different from mine. My mother has Native American blood on her side, and on my father's side there is southern white blood. Sometime back then my great-grandmother was taken advantage of by some plantation owner. My great-grandmother's family raised the baby; the white man couldn't be exposed. Despite some mixed blood here and there, as a kid I looked upon myself as just being black. The word "Afro-American" hadn't come into my vocabulary yet. Bobby Moore hadn't become Ahmad Rashad. Lew Alcindor hadn't become Kareem Abdul Jabar.

In South Africa having dinner in the home of this "black" family, I found they were considered by their society and by themselves to be "colored" — that is, of mixed races, and not black. These "coloreds" had a different legal status, a better place in South African society than blacks. After dinner they took me to a shantytown where the blacks lived. It was a real kind of education for me. This family, who to me were also black, were racist — racist toward the blacks of South Africa. They considered themselves "superior" to blacks, and, I discovered, were thought to have a higher status than people of pure African background. There was nothing in America so blatant as that. It shook me up for a while. I had discovered racism within my own race. That was new to me then. But I went on with my life, and only now as I read the racist letters being sent to me does that first visit to South Africa take on a whole new meaning.

Dear O.J.,

I have a question for you and your buddy A.C.
What do you think of "white trash" bitches who like to f—k rich n—rs now?

Ron Hendrickson
Reno, NV

Please come to Thanksgiving dinner. You may carve white meat.

[Anonymous]
Postmark: Boston, MA

Filthy Murdering N—ER MOTHER F—KER S.O.B. COKE HEAD

But you're not the only worthless n—er in this country. 98% of you are UNTERMENSCH S—T. The Ugliest species on the planet. UGLY HAIR, like wire, pig ears, primate noses, bulbous lips, and your ugly blackness. Unconscionable, irresponsible, dysfunctional, immoral, degenerate, perverted mother f—kers. The whole race is of the same kind.

You deserve the gas chamber.

[Anonymous]
Postmark: Belleville, IL

Until I read these obscene letters, I was sure this type of thinking had died in America in the sixties. By the time my own kids were born, I thought we would be further down the road. When I was age seven or eight, I was going by train with my family to Louisiana to visit relatives. When we got to Dallas, they made us pull the curtains shut all around our compartment in the railroad car we were riding in. Not all of us blacks were in one car — it was supposed to be an integrated car until we got to Texas! Then only a year or two later, my mother took me to march up Market Street in San Francisco with Martin Luther King, Jr. I marched and I heard him talk. He was everything to my mother. He was for being judged on merit alone. He reflected the philosophy I heard at Evergreen Baptist Church, where I was raised — do unto others as you would have others do unto you. It didn't take a grown-up to understand that Martin Luther King was against racism. He was larger than life, just like I felt emotionally that Jesus Christ was larger than life. Jesus also must have been against racism. King was our modern day Jesus Christ, and taught what Christ taught. He was the most important man in America because King's dream was that one day his four children would be judged by the content of their character and not by the color of their skin.

But it is still only a dream. That dream has not yet come true for anyone. I'm just exactly where I was some thirty years ago.

If the dream had come true, people would not have thought that Rodney King's beating was his own fault. They would have looked at that tape and seen it for what it was. King was no danger to anyone. He was reacting to getting his butt kicked. I've been around these types of fights as a kid. When I was a teenager I was once with my cousins and we were stopped by the police in San Francisco. We were searched and ended up being taken to the station. Some Laundromat had been robbed. I learned real quick that you have to become as docile as possible with the police. This was my first lesson on becoming docile around the police. I could have wound up pushed around like Rodney King was. My cousin was a little uppity and he ended up being roughed up.

Then there was the time when I was a little older that I stole some wine. We wanted it for a party. A friend of mine and some other boys ripped off some Orientals who owned this little store. We got busted. When we ran to the corner, the cops came around the corner to meet us. They were right on us. These two police officers put us up against the wall and I kept saying to A.C., who was the slowest of the group: "Let's run." I wouldn't have been caught, but I stayed with A.C. I became real docile again. My mother had to come and get me from the station. Twenty years later, I was stopped in Beverly Hills with Nicole. The cop claimed I had run a light. I hadn't, but I knew if I argued with him he probably would have ticketed me. I felt vulnerable. So once again I just became docile. And that time, I drove myself home.

Dear O.J.:

You were provoked, and as usual by a white person. White people are good for provoking one to violence. I know you've probably gotten thousands of letters to this effect but I just couldn't sit still and not let you know you have one more supporter out here.

Love ya!!

Audrey Lighter and Family
Sacramento, CA

Nobody should ever provoke anyone. To allow race to be an excuse for any provocation is simply wrong.

I decided not to make my life a no-win situation. I knew there were white people who would always see me as black, and black people who would see me as not black enough. I decided to do what I wanted to do and not let other people define my life. I would do my best with my abilities, and never allow my race to be used as a weapon against me.

Hi, O.J.,

Don't know why everyone is so surprised by your actions. I'm not. You were only following your old African instincts. You know, like that old saying goes: you can take the boy out of the jungle, but you can't take the jungle out of the boy. I want to thank you for slitting that white n—r's throat. All them bitches deserve the same thing. Feel sorry for that white dude though.

A fan of yours.

[Unsigned]
Postmark: Tampa, FL

Dear Mr. Simpson:

O.J., I don't have any facts at all on your history with Nicole. But why is it that whenever a Black man reaches the height of a successful venture of some sort he chooses to share that success and fame with a White woman? What was going on in your mind years ago when you started to cheat on your faithful wife for some 18-year-old White female? It was bad enough to cheat on her, but then you had to leave her for a younger, white blond. Oh, O.J. Now look at who's coming to your support—Black women! I'm amazed!!!! In case you don't know, a series of polls have been conducted regarding your guilt/innocence, and your biggest and most consistent supporter has been over-whelmingly the Black female — GO FIGURE!!!!!!!

So you see, you really screwed up by abandoning your own race of people to be with what you perceived to be better(?). You succumbed to what the media, and society told you was the epitome of beauty — the Blond.

Mr. Simpson, I personally have a lot going for me. I am college educated and very financially successful. I am also an African-American woman. I have not and will not stray from the Black man because I love, honor and respect him.

> *Good luck,*
>
> *Jacqueline Marquis*
> *Inglewood, CA*

Dear O.J.,

I have one question for you. Is it true that you don't like black women? Or should I say, we don't interest you romantically, or that you don't find us attractive? I'm curious. I await your reply.

My prayers and heart go out to you and especially
Sydney and Justin, during this trying time.

Sincerely,

Nadine Bynum
Norcross, GA

The press has created this image of me as being a playboy. As Marquerite and I were just splitting up, I met Nicole and we were together for the fifteen years. When I split up with Nicole in January of 1992, I wasn't looking for anybody. There were some other girls and there was one particular black girl that I was interested in, but I was trying to work things out with Nicole. One day a friend introduced me to another girl, a very spiritual girl. This was Paula. Except that they're both Caucasian, Nicole and Paula don't even look anything alike — Paula has dark hair. I was impressed with Paula's spiritualness and I needed some spiritualness in my life at the time. Earlier there was another girl that I was working with on the set of the TV series *First and Ten*. And she was a black woman, but I was married to Nicole at that time, so that didn't go any further. If I had met this black girl when Nicole and I were separated, who knows.

You warn your kids against candy and then some kids' teeth get cavities because of the candy. And you say: "I told you so." So it's like white America says a white woman shouldn't go out with a black guy, and blacks say you shouldn't go out with a white woman. When I was growing up I remember looking at all these great black women and seeing that they were with white guys. Diana Ross, Pearl Bailey, Lena Horne, and Leslie Uggams all seemed to be with white guys.

Some of white America is using me as an example of why white girls should not go out with black guys. They're saying blacks are inherently aggressive. I can see the jurors saying that also. Some of them, I'm sure, think blacks and Chicanos are inherently aggressive and violent. This racist thinking just never goes away.

Miss Bynum also sent me a copy of the *Washington Post* article which compares me to the classic Shakespeare story of Othello, "a brooding Moor in obsessive and ultimately fatal love with a white woman." What they're saying is that my life is about rage, envy, jealousy, and desire. I'm being portrayed as a wife-abuser and a violent person. This is not fair and is untrue.

The press says my trial may be the most important trial of a black man in America because it encompasses the basic principles that our Constitution was built on. And for someone who has never faced the racial issue head on, I'm now forced to confront the terrible truth about how the system creates racial issues, racial improprieties. Like the *Washington Post* story says: "O.J. Simpson has been accused of murder, and it makes you associate that likeness or that persona with that crime. That's the danger."

I grew up black. I grew up in a ghetto. It isn't like I wasn't aware of racism. I just chose not to let it define my life. I chose not to let it control me.

Part 3

Footprints in the Sand

Dear O.J.:

One night I had a dream. I was walking along the beach with the Lord, and across the skies flashed scenes from my life. After each scene, I noticed two sets of footprints in the sand. One was mine, and one was the Lord's. When the last scene of my life appeared before me, I looked back at the footprints in the sand, and, to my surprise, I noticed that many times along the path of my life there was only one set of footprints. And I noticed that it was at the lowest and saddest times in my life. I asked the Lord about it. "Lord, you said that once I decided to follow you, you would walk with me all the way. But I notice that during the most troublesome times in my life there is only one set of footprints. I don't understand why you left my side when I needed you most." The Lord said: "My precious child, I never left you during your time of trial. Where you see only one set of footprints, I was carrying you."

from

Wayne Lett and Family
Miami Shores, FL

I've received hundreds of letters where writers either wrote out these words, or enclosed a printed copy of these inspirational words, entitled "Footprints in the Sand."

Dear O.J.,

Please know that your life has brought years of pleasure to millions of us— that cannot be wiped away. Please know, too, that there are a great many Christians who, by nature, will continue to be in prayer for you. As followers of Jesus Christ it is not for us to judge you, only to love you and to forgive your human frailties, as Christ continually does for each of His children.

Please be in prayer for yourself, as well. Pray for forgiveness, strength, and peace and believe they are yours. Ask the Lord, Jesus Christ, into your life and give Him the control of its outcome.

Well, you may never read this letter but I feel better for having written it. God bless you, my brother in Christ.

> *In His Love,*
> *Carole Proudfoot*
> *Overland Park, KS*

Mr. O.J. Simpson,

Hello. My name is Keyon and I'm 14. I think that you didn't do it, but if you did it will be something you

*and God work out. Remember that God will all
ways forgive you for what ever you do. All you have to do
is ask. I know that it is hard for you to sleep in that jail
cell. There is a lesson to be learned from everything you
do good and bad. Mr. Simpson, don't give up and I hope
that everything comes together.*

Sincerely,

*Keyon Haynes
Seagirt Beach, NY*

This tragedy has changed my relationship with God, how I relate to God. I think about God a lot now. I do believe that God was trying to get my attention and this trouble is God's way of getting my attention. And He has gotten my attention.

The first week I was in jail I thought about Jesus being crucified. I thought about what I was going through. But then I said to myself I had kids — that made the difference. I prayed. I might have been suicidal that first week. I just wanted it to end. I prayed numerous times. I begged God to just take me, to let me be with Nicole.

Anyone who knows me knows that I'm innocent, knows that I didn't do this. I sat in my cell during the first week and I prayed to God. I told Him: I am not up to whatever it is I'm being asked to do now. I'm not up to it. I prayed for my life to end. And then I realized I had no choice. I had no choice but to endure because I've got kids. I had no choice but to endure.

Dear O.J.,

I want to encourage you in Jesus Christ.

It's our belief, O.J., that God has His hand upon your life and God wants to use you for His Glory!!

And we are holding you up in sincere, heartfelt prayers and we are praying for all your attorneys also!! Your Family too!!!

There's power in Prayer!!

In Christ's love.

Elizabeth Gossett
Palm Desert, CA

When this all started I got down on my knees and prayed to God. In the first cell I was placed in, I prayed to God on my knees. It's hard for me to pray that way for the floor is all cement and I have bad knees from my football days. I even tried to take some weight off my knees by putting my arms on the toilet. It was so awkward to do that. My first cell was so small, the only place I could pray was in front of the toilet stool. But I'm now in a different cell where I can't even do that. The only place to pray is in bed. Now I sit up in bed or I lie in bed to pray. I don't know if it's all that important what position I'm in, just so long as I pray.

There's times, now that I am in jail, that all I have is God.

God has brought me so much closer than I've ever been to what's really important in life: I look at all my kids and God's given me the answer to life.

I think I also probably have a better understanding of my need for God in my life now. I recognize the need I have to have God in my life. Maybe I've always felt that I was on God's side. I knew God was on everybody's side. But I always felt that if I was to be judged by anyone, I would have to live by God's rule, "do unto others" — you know, the Golden Rule. That was the philosophy that was rooted in the Evergreen Baptist Church I went to, as a boy in San Francisco. It's "do unto others as you would have others do unto you." You went there and you learned about Jesus. But it was my mother who first taught me to "do unto others." I remember going with her and giving my first speech to anyone — it was at church and it was Easter. I had to speak in front of about 250 members of the congregation. It was about "do unto others" and I almost forgot it that time. That was the last time I'd ever forget it.

For that reason I never felt afraid of life. A lot of people are guarded because they feel threatened. I had never really felt this way. It's a self-assurance that comes from my mother's teaching me the Golden Rule.

Dear O.J.

Dear brother in Jesus Christ, perhaps by now you feel your life is like Job in the Old Testament. Remember Job's story had a happy ending.

*God's ways are mysterious. But I know that if you
will turn your life over to God and completely rededicate
your life to Jesus you will see miracles. I believe in my
heart where you are today you have no other options.
God is always talking to us, sometimes we just don't listen.*

In His Love,

*Sarah Nichols Brown
Malibu, CA*

I get so many letters that ask me if I've read Job. I was really
unaware of all that Job went through, how he had everything
stripped from him to test his faith in God. I, myself, went
through a phase in jail when all these things began to happen
to me. Now I am able to relate to Job.

After about a week and a half in here I started reading Job. I
finished Job and then I got athlete's foot. I never had athlete's
foot in my life. But I got it so bad that the deputies had to
bring in a solution for me to soak my feet in, some type of
brine. I had a bad reaction to the solution. My feet swelled up
and not only did I have fungus growing, I had blisters and
everything. One bad thing led to another. I felt like Job with
the broken pottery, sitting in the ashes of his home, scratching
his boils. The boils of Job.

I kept saying to myself: It's almost like when you reach a point and it can't get any worse. Before this I would have never thought about the Bible in a personal way. What you find in the Bible is that you're not the first, you're not the first person this happened to. You find also that you weren't the first person that's been totally emotionally crushed, or felt that everything was against you.

So Satan went out from the presence of the Lord and struck Job with a terrible case of boils from head to foot.

(Job 2: 7)

My skin is filled with worms and blackness. My flesh breaks open, full of pus. My life flies by— day after hopeless day. My life is but a breath, and nothing good is left.

(Job 7: 5-7)

But now my grief remains no matter how I defend myself; nor does it help if I refuse to speak. For God has ground me down, and taken away my family. O God, you have turned me to skin and bones— as a proof, they say, of my sins. God hates me and angrily tears at my flesh; he has gnashed

upon me with his teeth, and watched to snuff out
any sign of life.
(Job 16: 6-9)

My enemies gather themselves against me. And
God has delivered me over to sinners, into the
hands of the wicked.
(Job 16: 10-11)

I was living quietly until he broke me apart. He
has taken me by the neck and dashed me to pieces,
then hung me up as his target. His archers sur-
round me, letting fly their arrows, so that the
ground is wet from my wounds. Again and again,
he attacks me, running upon me like a giant. Here
I sit in sackcloth; and have laid all hope in the
dust. My eyes are red with weeping and on my eye-
lids is the shadow of death. Yet I am innocent and
my prayer is pure....
(Job 16: 12-17)

In all of this, Job did not sin or revile God.
(Job 42: 1)

...the Lord restored his wealth and happiness! In
fact, the Lord gave him twice as much as before!
(Job 42: 10)

So the Lord blessed Job at the end of his life more than at the beginning.

(Job 42: 12)

Then there are the Psalms, which say so much. Psalm 31. These verses really, really hit home for me. Psalm 31 was one of the first things I found in the Bible. I read it to Rosie Grier, who came to pray with me in those first days. And then Rosie went out and tried to read it to the press. But his Bible was the King James version and I had the "Living Letter" version that my attorney and friend Robert Kardashian had given to me during his first visit with me in jail. I like reading Psalm 31:

"Lord, I trust in you alone." I just love reading from the Bible now. "Lord, I trust in you alone. Don't let my enemies defeat me. Rescue me because you are the God who always does what is right. Answer quickly when I cry to you."

I also like this part: "O Lord, have mercy on me, in my anguish. My eyes are red from weeping." These were all part of the things I was relating to. "My health is broken from sorrow. I am pining away with grief; my years are shortened, drained away because of sadness." This is exactly what I was feeling that first week in jail. I mean my feet were swollen, I had blisters, I was grieving, I had lost Nicole.

"My sins have sapped my strength; I stoop with sorrow and with shame. I am scorned by all my enemies and even more by my neighbors and friends." Well, not all my friends.

"They dread meeting me and look the other way when I go by." That's what I was feeling that first week. No matter what happens, there are people who are going to be skeptical of me. For as long as I live, there are people who are going to be skeptical of me, who are going to dread meeting me.

Again it says: "I heard the lies about me, the slanders of my enemies. Everywhere I looked I was afraid, for they were plotting against my life."

All of these things I can relate to so much now. At the end of Psalm 31 it says: "Oh, love the Lord, all of you who are his people; for the Lord protects those who are loyal to him, but harshly punishes all who haughtily reject him. So cheer up! Take courage if you are depending on the Lord." This gave me more than hope, it showed me that someone else had been where I am at, at a place where the writer in the Bible is accused of doing some horrible thing and everybody is pointing at him and people are plotting against him.

In those first weeks I felt like this couldn't happen to anybody; nobody could go through what I was going through. But now what I really think is somebody else has gone through it. I'm taken away from my loved ones and people are plotting against me, people are lying about me and here it all is in the Bible. What the Lord has given me is the Word of God, the word that there's nothing that I could suffer that the Lord didn't know. I know now He wouldn't give me any more than I could handle.

Dear Mr. Simpson,

I believe from what I have heard, that you were brought up by a mother who sounds like a Christian woman.

If you have never personally asked Jesus to come into your heart and life and to save you— please, please do. Please listen to Rosie Grier and Vince Evans when they talk about the Lord.

"Doing unto others" is a great way of life, but it of itself won't get us into Heaven. Even though we've never met, I love you, and am praying for you.

In Christ,

Jerry Payne
Wingate, NC

As the weeks and months pass, the letters I get are definitely more spiritual. At first I got letters because of my football career, my acting, and some just out of curiosity. My mother made this clear to me; that what God intended for me is that I've always had an audience, but at this point, now my audience is a much more serious audience. It's a much more spiritual audience. Now most of the people who are writing to me haven't written to me ever before. Half of them must not even have really followed my career either in football or the movies. The letters I get now have a much more spiritual feeling and I feel in many ways connected to them.

———————————

Dear Mr. Simpson,

I am pastor at little church in Pompano Beach, Florida.

The reason this is happening to you is that God is trying to talk to you. God is going to make you a leader and just as you were a role model for the world you will be a role model in the name of our Lord and Savior Jesus Christ.

Your sister in Christ,

Evangelist Bernice Washington
Ft. Lauderdale, FL

———————————

Dear O.J.,

I just wanted to drop you a few lines to let you know that people still believe in you and love you.

I hope you will read this letter and find the encouragement to go on. I believe God has guided you from the projects to being a superstar and he will not desert you now.

This is the time to count your blessings. Take care of yourself and remember millions of people are praying for you. You remain in my thoughts and prayers.

> *Sincerely,*
> *Gloria Breault*
> *Chicago, IL*

Dear O.J. Simpson:

I just want you to know that I'm one of the multitudes who has great faith in you, and I'm praying for you every day, and during the day.

God ever bless you, and strengthen you.

> *Your fan and friend*
>
> *Anna L. Mondragon*
> *Union City, CA*

As I've said, Paula is a very spiritual person. During the first month and a half I was in jail, all we talked about was Scripture. During my conversations with her, I came to the realization that when I'm out of here, even though I'm not a preacher—I can't preach—I have to share what happened because when I read these letters and I read between the lines, I see how many people are hurting out there. I think if this could happen to me, it could happen to anybody. If it wasn't for the Bible, that I now have at all times with me, I don't know if I'd survive. There is hope. Psalm 31 gave me hope. Job gave me hope. Psalm 86 gave me hope: "Protect me from death, for I try to follow all your laws. Save me, for I am serving you and trusting you. Be merciful, O Lord, for I am looking up to you in constant hope." (Psalm 86: 2-3)

Material witnesses like Paula and others who have been my friends over the years come to see me in jail and they share life with me. They also have a need for me. If these witnesses weren't also my true friends, I couldn't stand to have them come down to see me in jail. I couldn't stand to be a burden on these people.

Then there are the "friends." That's where I relate to Jesus in the Bible. Can you imagine when Pontious Pilate and all those people, when all the witnesses were coming forward saying things about Him? Reading about the peace that He had — He certainly had more strength than I have. I think: How did He handle it? They made Him guilty. He had to sit there and listen to these Judases. How could these people live with Jesus and still, when it came time to have faith and show their faith in support of Him, they weren't able to do it? So here I am, almost two thousand years later, and I have to have faith in Him. I hope you can see what I am trying to say. I look at Faye Resnick, who wants to say she was part of my inner sanctum, but she wasn't. So she's not a Judas to me because Faye was just an acquaintance. She's just bearing false witness. What annoys me about Faye is that Faye has done this to Nicole. Not me. Nicole's the one who's not here to defend herself against those lies. How could anyone do these things to Nicole? Anyone who claims she was her "close" friend?

What keeps me going now is my children and my new-found faith.

Dear O.J.,

I'm sorry for what happened to you, and I pray for you and your family. I believe you didn't do it, and if you have faith and believe in God you can get through this. Please don't take your life, it's not worth it, you got a lot to live for. (1) Your self, (2) your kids, (3) your mom. So I'll light a candle for you and pray every day that God helps you and guides you.

Bill Juarez
Mira Loma, CA

I know that I will raise my children differently in relationship to God. Without a doubt. I can visualize it. I have already visualized it every Sunday. I won't play golf. Sunday we will go to church, and on Sundays I will expose them to more than just the Catholic church in my neighborhood.

Nicole raised them Catholic, but they don't know what's

going on when they go to church. I'll take them to Johnnie Cochran's church, the Second Baptist Church near downtown L.A. I'm going to take them because their congregation is black and white. I realize now I've got to show them all of their heritage. My first two children had so much exposure to the world, because I was playing football and I lived an integrated life. They saw both sides of the street. Arnelle and Jason grew up in a white neighborhood, but they had so much exposure to the black community that they have had no problems. They know both societies and both social structures. I don't want Sydney and Justin raised only in Laguna Beach, because that's a predominantly white community and that's only one part of their heritage. I want them exposed to all facets of not only religion but race as well. In Laguna Beach they won't have the balance that is needed. I want to expose my kids to Christianity as a whole and let them gravitate to what parts of it they want to gravitate to. What's important is that Sydney and Justin have the Lord in their lives. Now they have a little religious training once a week, something they do at church. They are doing fine for now, but in the future they've got to be exposed to more. I know what a difference God can make.

Dear Mr. Simpson,

You ran away from the scene of the crime, you ran away (the coward) from the police but you can't run away from

yourself and God. The Bible says God will one day make
all things known.

   Ecclesiastes
   Chapter 12, verse 14

         [Unsigned]
         Postmark: Topeka, KS

Once again the ugly letters and once again they don't sign it. If somebody doesn't sign it, I cannot, no matter what it says, in terms of religion or otherwise, respond. I won't increase their presence. If they won't sign their letters they lack real conviction and integrity. One can only question their true faith.

Family

My mother often came down from San Francisco to L.A. to spend a week with us. She always sat on my tennis court in the backyard while I would read the paper and drink my juice. She loved the backyard because there were lots of hummingbirds around.

❧

This family photograph was taken some twelve years ago in San Francisco. From left to right you have me, my sister, Shirley, and my mother, Eunice. Then there is my younger sister, Carmelita, my dad, Jimmie, and my older brother, Truman. On the left is a picture of my dad with Sydney just before he died in 1986.

🖎

Christmas in New York, the Big Apple. From left to right we have Michele, Jason's girlfriend; sorry, I don't remember who's in the Santa outfit. There are Lou and Judy Brown and just below

❧

them are Denise with her son, and my daugther Sydney. There's Nicole and me with our son Justin, then there's my older son, Jason. Below them are Tanya and Dominique with her son Randy.

Nicole was big on taking pictures. We always had a camera with us, and over the sixteen years you can see our whole life and the life of our kids. Here are a few of the times Sydney and Justin had their friends over and the camera was there.

Here Jason is wearing my LAPD cap. He's about ten and Arnelle is twelve. This picture was taken at my Rockingham home, back when I supported the LAPD.

Where I Am

Dear O.J.

I met you in 1979 after one of your last games with the 49ers. I was just 18 years old and it was such an honor and thrill for me! I vividly remember your beautiful smile and magical spirit. I'm so glad to see your smile again as I see brief news reports. I'll never forget how polite you were to me on that cold day and when you spoke to me and signed an autograph, it warmed my soul. I think of you and your family daily and wish you all the best and the strength to get through this tough time. My best wishes are with you.
A true fan.

Sincerely,
Jeanne Gould
San Mateo, CA

Dear Mr. Simpson,
Several years ago my wife and I had the pleasure and honor of meeting you. You spoke to and treated us as if

we were friends of yours. You were very friendly and cordial and we will never forget that. The autograph you gave us hangs proudly and always will in our living room.

Peace and God Bless You,

Kenneth Thrun

Buffalo, NY

I can recall many times rushing for airplanes, especially during the years I worked for NBC as an announcer. Some lady sees me and comes running after me. Maybe her son is a few feet back, because he's shy, but he's your biggest fan, she says; he has your picture. As his mother's running after me, she's telling me all this. And I'm literally sprinting to try to make a flight. These are the times when I feel bad because I can't stop and talk to the kid; I can't stop and sign the photograph. Now if this family follows me, I'll sign whatever I can sign for them when I'm at the gate. There have been so many times I've sat on a plane and felt so bad that the family didn't follow me to the gate and that I wasn't able to stop and do my thing. Being gracious was my thing.

In the past, there have been only a few times when I felt overwhelmed by the demands of the fans. The first time it really hit me was when I was still in college. I was in New York City and I had just won the Heisman Trophy. Marquerite was expecting our first child, like the day of the presentation. The Downtown Athletic Club of New York City who awarded me this honor had me on such a heavy publicity schedule—TV shows, luncheons, meetings—and then in between were all the people, all the well-wishers. I needed a nap.

It was the first time in my life I can remember where I just couldn't get enough sleep. But I felt this great responsibility to the public. I had been raised to be gracious. But for the first time in my life, time did not allow me to be gracious. I felt bad, it bothered me, and I must admit, when I finally did get time to rest, I was fitful and could not sleep.

Mr. Simpson,

I was able to see your sweet mother and sister on TV. You are blessed with a wonderful family. Your son and daughter were wonderful on the interview I saw with NBC *Dateline. I think [smile symbol] I know the blessing of a wonderful family. To me, the most important people in one's life are his family and good friends.*

Keep your chin up, O.J.

Someone who cares.
Jewel Chadd Broadfoot
Shawnee, KS

My mother raised all us kids in a loving home. We lived in a government housing project in San Francisco and you had to get along with everybody. If you had a "roach" problem, those little cockroaches, you couldn't solve it just in your home alone. The whole eight families or however many were in the building had to work together to solve that problem. You had to work with people. I was influenced by that at a real early age. If you were gracious, you got a lot done. Sometimes the message was indirect and sometimes the message on how to get along with people was very direct.

In '58, when I was almost eleven, the Giants came to San Francisco. I was actually playing baseball and some football. Everybody was talking about this guy I had never seen, Willie Mays. I didn't know who Willie Mays was. All the white teachers in school seemed to get just as excited about Mays and the Giants as my mother or my uncle Hollis did. And all of a sudden, I realized he was a black man. People smiled when they talked about him. There was so much joy and adulation when people talked about Willie Mays. I first saw him at the second game the Giants played. I left school without official permission, and just went over to Seals Stadium, less than a mile from school. I spotted him playing right away. You could see this guy was something special. I mean, when Willie Mays hit three homers it was like I hit three homers! He just became my alter ego. He became my hero. But I didn't meet him until I was a teenager.

That was at the time I got in trouble with A.C. and another friend, and my mother had to come and get me from the police station. When something happens in the community, everybody knows. It's like the drum beats. Somebody gets shot, somebody gets arrested, and it's like a PA system starts broadcasting. Even though my mom and dad were divorced, I knew my mom would call my dad and he'd show up. I waited for him to give me a whipping. I was asleep, maybe at about 4:30 in the afternoon, and I heard this talking downstairs. So I knew my dad was there. Then my mother called in this funny, real high voice she never used when I was about to be punished: "Orenthal, come down."

I knew my dad wasn't there to whip me.

I came downstairs and there was Willie Mays. This guy named Lefty Gordon, who was the director at the Booker T. Washington Center, heard over the "PA system" about what happened. He knew I was in trouble, and he knew Mays, and he convinced Willie to come to my house. I ended up spending the day with Willie. I went with him to the cleaners before they closed, and his stuff wasn't ready. It was the weirdest thing to me. It was Willie Mays and his stuff wasn't ready. But Willie was gracious about it. Then he took me to his house where they were preparing for some kind of banquet. I remember the winding staircase and I thought, This is unbelievable. He had this $80,000 house. Now, this was the early sixties — a house like that would cost millions today. It was the first time I saw the pot of gold at the end of the rainbow. Now that I think back, it was the first time I saw generosity and greatness up close.

I wasn't much smaller than him. I was almost as fast as he was. I noticed he was just a regular guy. He was human. He didn't speak any better than I did. But he was almost a god. He was already my alter ego. I remember that I didn't get his autograph; I didn't need to. I had him inside of me.

It was a nice day. And I learned a lesson from it. I realized that if this guy could make it, I could make it. I don't think that after that day I ever got into any trouble.

Dear O.J.,

   Please hang in there and trust in God and I have faith
everything will turn out fine. If you really knew how many

people loved you, I think it would give you strength. I
admired the gallant way in which you took the news.

You indeed are one of a kind.

B.J. Rogers
Johnstown, PA

I started to learn that your best lessons come through adversity.
After going to the University of Southern California and playing
great football, a sport that I got serious about in junior college,
I had the good fortune of having the misfortune of going to
Buffalo to play football. In this day and age, who would go to
Buffalo? The system says the last-place team gets to pick the top
player in the draft. And that is what happened. I was the first
pick and Buffalo got me. I wanted to play for a West Coast
team. But what you have to do is go and do it. I never com-
plained. I made the best of it and didn't try to find an easy way
out. When you do your best, you have no regrets. In the years
I played there, the Bills still had a losing record. But nobody
ever looked upon me as a loser. I never, never, felt like a loser.
Buffalo may have been a little behind in some ways, but there
was one thing about Buffalo that stayed with me. They had
hardworking people and you had to earn their respect by the
way you played the game. In L.A., if you drive a good-looking
car, you're respected. In Buffalo, you had to earn respect. I have
always liked people who've earned what they've got.

Dear O.J.,

> *I just want you to know that all of us here in Buffalo
> are pulling for you. I especially am praying for you every
> day. Please hang tough. Everything will work out in the
> end if you believe in yourself, and I know millions of peo-
> ple believe in you. I know you will be found innocent. I
> thought I would send you a copy of the picture you took
> with myself, my brother, and my cousin seven months ago,
> the night before you were honored along with the Electric
> Company at Rich Stadium. It is something I will always
> cherish and remember.*

> > *God Bless You, Juice!!!*
> > *Good Luck,*
> >
> > *Paul Tomasello*
> > *Cheektowaga, NY*

When I left football, only one year after I returned to San
Francisco to play for the 49ers, I left a legacy. Everybody who
played with me, and everybody who played against me, enjoyed
it. Everybody who played with me understood that I loved
playing football. I wanted to leave a legacy: Here's a guy who
did it the right way, who played by the rules, showed good
sportsmanship, fair play, competed as hard as he could com-
pete. Then when the game was over, they would say, "Hey,
O.J., wasn't that a good match?"

O.J. —

My heart hurts for you.

Unfortunately, you people who are our sports legends have become our idols. Even tho I am not a thorough sports advocate, even I know of your notoriety in the sports world and you have been and still are being idolized. Idols are somehow perceived as individuals who never fail nor disappoint us — how untrue this is, especially, of those idols, which are flesh and blood, with the capacity to go from very low to very high and uncontrollable surges of emotional behavior.

Sincerely,
Shirley Ann Haney
Reedley, CA

Dear Mr. Simpson,

Just because you are incarcerated doesn't make you any less of a man. Use this time wisely and institute the inner strength you possess, to overcome this trial and tribulation. Don't let it overwhelm you, you have overcome barriers before, and this is just another to overcome. It may be higher than those before, but it can be dealt with sucessfully.

Sincerely your friend,
R.J. (Rick) Lewis
Lakeland, FL

Since that day with Willie Mays I was always in control of my life. The last event I had full control of was when I walked into a Chicago airport hotel, the O'Hare Plaza hotel, the morning of June 13 last summer. There was nobody in the lobby, but as I arrived at the desk, there was this guard and these two people behind the desk, and they were waiting for an autograph.

Then, within hours, my life got away from me.

Now I sit in my jail cell unjustly accused of something I did not do. As I read all these letters, I realize that so many of these people who write to me have a positive image of me, but they really don't seem to know much about my career. They've heard my name, but have not really followed my career either in sports or as a sports announcer.

I now have to live by new rules. The greatest thing sports tells you is how to work within a system. How to work with people. Now I am in jail, and jail has its own rules. For the first time, I was totally in other people's hands.

When I first came in here, I was so deep inside myself, dealing with the enormity of what had happened. This is probably the first time in my life that I was inside myself to that extent. The best thing that happened to me was I got angry. I was being accused of two deaths that I did not cause. As I said before, I know this anger brought me out of my grief, and out of my fog. And once I started getting angry, I started getting stronger and stronger.

There is something wrong with the jail system when it comes to holding prisoners like me, who are only accused and have no criminal record. After all, we are supposed to be presumed innocent. The system is wrong to treat me exactly like a convicted criminal in this place when I'm still innocent under the law. I'm led everywhere in handcuffs and a body chain. I have to kowtow when I'm told: "Stand here," "Stand there," "Face the wall" — you know. A lot of what they do makes sense to me for convicted criminals. But even the legal system seems to ignore the presumption of innocence. I'm being treated like the worst criminal in the place, but I'm sure learning more about the law.

There are about eleven sheriff's deputies working in my area of the jail. These guys are real professionals. I hope I have not made their jobs any more difficult than what they normally are. They have rules, and I know how to live by the rules: when you eat, when you shower, when you change your clothes. After I'm released, I'm going to have a weekly golf tournament with a rotating group of deputies. I must say I'm impressed with the sheriff's department — at least the people running this place. They're totally professional — not like the LAPD.

Dear Mr. Simpson:

> *How are you? You are looking better.*
> *You need to keep your mental strength up and hold yourself together. You have a lot of people who love you and will continue to love no matter what.*
> *Remember this is only a detour.*
>
> > *Sincerely,*
> >
> > *Linda Lewis and Family*
> > *Glendale, AZ*

Whatever my past was I know. I don't know about my future as I answer these letters in this book. I do know that when I'm low, my friends pull me up, and when I'm too high, they pull me down a little. You need to hold yourself together. Allow those who love you to stand by you. Don't let them down. I look around this jail and I see others who have the strength to live under incarceration. I think I'm as strong as these other guys. Besides that, I have the strength of being innocent.

Dear O.J.,

You are looking as though you are sleeping better. Make sure you eat really good. I know when I'm down if I eat nutritious foods it helps. What kinds of food are they serving you? Do you have any choices?

It seems your press coverage is messing up the soaps. I think that's great, I hate the soaps. I'm so curious as to what your day consists of.

Till next time,

Kim Weisenberger
Mooresville, NC

I don't like what's on TV. In jail all I see is the negative and the misery of man. They set the channel to and I'm forced to watch shows like *Beverly Hills 90210* and stuff like that. Take a good look at these shows and you will see that the most popular people on these shows are the ones that are contriving and conniving and that goes back to the days of J.R. on *Dallas*. That says something about TV in here and its values. They're not my values.

I sleep all right and it's warm enough in here. I try to eat what I'm given, but I'm still losing weight. On the days when I go to court, which is most days, I was getting what is called a "court line sandwich" for dinner, which is the same sandwich I have for lunch. Just a piece of bologna or some other lunch meat on two pieces of bread. Plus some cookies or maybe an apple. There is no way anyone can stay healthy eating that twice a day, and then eating these high-cholesterol eggs and potatoes they give me in the morning, which half the time are cold. I can't get anything from the outside. Now at least I get a hot meal at night when I return from court, but it took a court order signed by the judge.

The worst thing is trying to get motivated in jail. Whenever I work out, I get rushes of energy. So now I can't work out, because I don't want to get rushes of energy when I'm in my cell. Right now, I'm probably three or four pounds underweight. Every once in a while, I see myself reflected in something as I'm going to court. I saw myself one day last month and for the first time in my life I felt that I was getting older. I said to myself: It's taking its toll. Maybe it was my spirit that was older—I've always had a young spirit. I was a brother, a friend, to my older children. Now I noticed that I am older. It was the first time in my life that I really saw that I was getting near fifty. I looked fifty and I felt fifty. I've never been there before.

Dear O.J.,

    *I decided that just letting you know that you and
your family will continue to be in my prayers may be all
I can do but it is important to let you know you are not
alone— many people believe in you and will continue to
support you— don't give up!*

    *As time passes, it is very important for you to remem-
ber that you will make it through and although no one
can say when— you will be with your family again and
you will be able to move on. Sometimes we forget to focus
on the real goal and things seem impossible— You can't
let yourself think that way— Remember obstacles are just
things we see when we take our eyes off of our goal.*

                      Take One Day At A Time.

          J. Diane Karlin
          King of Prussia, PA

I'm so alone for the first time in my life. I'm in isolation all the time. I haven't had one full conversation with another person except when I have visitors. I have good days and I have days when I get so disillusioned. They say I'm in solitary confinement for my own good. I wonder about that. Solitary in here doesn't mean you're really alone. I have two video cameras watching me all the time. At first I got flat-out indignant because I could not even go to the toilet without these cameras watching me. The pictures go to some office somewhere. I don't know the kind of people viewing those pictures of me. Maybe there are female officers in there. It took a couple of days, but now the video cameras are not pointed toward the toilet in my cell.

O.J. Simpson:

> *Always remember:*
> *He who loses money, loses much:*
> *He who loses a friend, loses more:*
> *But he who loses courage, loses all.*

> > *A friend,*
> >
> > *Shauna S. Baugh*
> > *Decatur, GA*

Hi, O.J.,

> *The course of our lives are not ours to do as we desire. Every incident that takes place has a reason no matter how small. There are a great amount of things taking place at this moment involving the public, which has to come to the awareness of the people of this world. Never before in history has something like this taken place before.*
>
> *Keep in mind at all times, you were chosen, O.J. Only a special person could have been chosen. You are*

special. You may not see this clearly. Remember there is a
light at the end of the tunnel. After the storm there is a
calm. Your life will continue and be stronger than ever.
Believe me it will.

For there is hope for a tree, if it be cut down, that it
will sprout again. Job 14: 7

> *Bye for now.*
> *Love and Sincerity,*
> *Jacintha Cindy Campbell*
> *Huntington, NY*

Today I don't know if I am a better man because of this experience I'm having. I think eventually I will be, but today as I write this book, I'm not. But eventually I will be. When I get rid of the negative feelings I have in me, I will be a better man. I never had these feelings in me before. I do have a better understanding of life versus death. I have a better feel for what's important, really important in life.

My whole life has been one of "I paid the price." I mean there is one thing you can say about O.J.: O.J. wasn't given anything. I worked hard for everything I got. I paid the price for everything, and I owned up to everything, even when I thought I was getting the short end of the stick, whether it was my personal life or my football career. But I ask myself over and over and over: If I'm innocent, why should I pay any price?

I do know that I have to share with the world what has happened in here. I will write my autobiography, the full story of my life. But even before I do that, I must share this experience. If this injustice could happen to me, it could happen to anybody. I'm not a preacher, but I have a lot to preach about now.

O.J.,

Take care and keep yourself in good shape for the day you are in the arms of your two children again.

Keep the Faith

Marylou
Postmark: Royal Oak, MI

It may be hard for anyone to understand what it is like not to be able to touch a person you love for six months or more. I have not been able to physically, actually, touch a single person I love. I'm a loving guy. I love my sons and my daughters, my younger kids and my older children. We are all huggers. It was one of the rituals with my son Justin every morning. He would run in and jump on me in bed and give me this big hug, show me how hard he could hug. It was a ritual in my family. I have not had a hug in almost seven months.

Loving Memories

What more could I say about Christmas at home? Here are Justin and Sydney in the den of my home on Rockingham Drive. I just love this little picture.

This was the year we went to Yosemite. I took the kids boating and fishing and we did a lot of horseback riding. That's Sydney on the

❧

pony and Justin and Sydney next to one of the inflatable rafts. We rent-
ed a mobile home. Nicole pitched the tents, and I did the cooking.

❧

Every year I had a Fourth of July party at my home. We never invited fewer than 300 of our friends and family, kids and adults alike. Everyone who was invited was thrown into the swimming pool as part of the yearly ritual. That's Nicole on my back some years ago. It was an all-day and all-night affair, with lots of food and music.

During the Fourth of July party, all of us guys have a softball game. Look at the faces and you will see almost every sport, from basket-ball to football. The wonderful thing is that we really like to play the game. On the right I am just having fun in the Caribbean.

The picture was taken at Las Brisas restaurant high above Laguna Beach, California. My mother, Eunice, is with Dominique and Nicole. Nicole has Justin, and Dominique's son Aaron is in the stroller with Sydney.

What It's All About

In Care of O.J. Simpson:

To O.J.'s Mom,

Dearest Mom;

    Ever since this horrible event happened I have been praying without ceasing.
    I know your son did not do these horrible crimes. I know you've worried about him, as all mothers do. And you've burned the midnight oil praying.
    I am praying for the families of the victims as well. That God would hold their hands now, and reserve judgment until he reveals who has been the real guilty party. There has been a terrible loss here, and grief does many things, so be patient and understanding.

          Stand steadfast.

          Charlene Carlisle
          California

Every kid in my neighborhood wanted my mom to be theirs. My mother is the greatest mom because of who she is. Our house was where all my friends came, where everybody came. My father moved out when I was four, and my mother never remarried. She was kind of a single parent. But my father stayed in touch. He didn't remarry either. He always came for Thanksgiving, for Christmas. And he was always around when he was needed — he wasn't far away. He was there to give me a whipping when I needed one.

My mother was spiritual, not a strict disciplinarian. She was not what some people would call a "power player." She spoke to us kids harshly sometimes, but only when we were wrong. My sisters Shirley and Carmelita, and my brother, Truman, never really talked back to my mom: we just knew she was right. She never gave us any crap and we never gave her any. If you were out of line she told you, and you knew it — you knew you'd been told. But she didn't have to tell us we were out of line very often.

Missus Simpson, as my mother was called by the kids in the neighborhood, always worked in a hospital. My mother was never on welfare. She worked her whole life. She's seventy-four now and she retired when she was sixty-five. When I started making money, I started sending her a check every month. I didn't miss a month. Then two years later, I'm sitting with my personal adviser, Skip Taft, and my accountant one day, and they are going over the books. Skip makes this little comment, says something about my mother. It seems that the checks I keep sending have never come back to the bank. Am I sending them to the correct address or what? That night I called my mother and said: "You're messing up my checking account." And she tells me she has all my checks. She wasn't cashing them because she was saving the money for me. She thought I would need it one day. She was a working lady; she was fending for herself. All of her kids were doing for themselves. After my call, she cashed the checks.

But my sister Shirley tells me that all the money is still sitting in a separate account. You know, my mom came from a time where she heard about Joe Louis and his problems with losing all his money. It was just her way. She was just putting the money away for her kid.

My mother did not have a thirties depression mentality. She grew up okay. She went to school in Shreveport. Went to Central Colored High School and got her nursing credentials. There were a lot of kids in her family and they lived on something like one hundred acres. They were relatively well off; nobody grew up with holes in his jeans and neither did I.

Dear O.J.,

I know you know God because forty-six years ago Mrs. Simpson taught you and brought you up to believe in the Almighty God. Why? Because it's our heritage and our culture. I hope you read the poem "Footprints," because it's God who is carrying you now and will all the way from now on if only you believe.

I am,

Ms. Georgia K. Thomas

Marshall, TX

When I was young, I held it against my father for a lot of years that he and my mother split. As I said before, not until Marguerite and I split did I realize that it wasn't necessarily all my dad's fault. He and my mother reached a point when it was time for them to go down different paths. It was the same with Nicole and me. We reached the same point.

After I got too old for my dad to give me whippings and after I started playing football at USC, he came to a few games. We were still in our noncommunicative period — I was still upset that he had left my mother. But he attended all the big games and was always supportive of me. In the end we got together. He was cooking all the time with Nicole, and made his annual pilgrimage to us at the holidays. We got closer before he died in 1986, during the years he knew he had cancer.

One day in 1986, I woke up in bed with Nicole and just said to her: "I feel like I got to go see my dad." I wanted to go see him. It was like the weirdest thing. I flew up to San Francisco and planned to spend the day with my mom, and then see my dad at his place, since I was going on the road shortly. I went to my momma's house first and nobody was there. I knew one of my sisters was staying with my dad, so I went by his house and nobody was there either. I called Nicole and she says: "Where are you? Your dad's at the hospital." I went to the hospital and my whole family was there. I just walked in and kind of put my hand on his, and he kind of gave me a squeeze, and he said: "I thought you weren't going to make that flight." He liked teasing me about the Hertz commercials where it seemed that I was always late — my dad was like that. I sat there and held his hand, and my mother was sitting in the room with him and I said: "Let me call Nicole: she's worried." I went to the pay phone on the floor and I wasn't on the phone a minute and my sister came running out — "You gotta come!" I ran back into the room and my dad was dead. I don't know why God gave me that five minutes for my dad and not a second for Nicole. It hurts so much about Nicole, I don't know why God didn't give me time with her.

Throughout this part of our conversation O.J. became emotional. His voice broke a few times, and then he wept.

Nicole always used to always say to me even after we split, "I love you." And I'd say back, "I love you." We tried to say these things whenever we parted because you just never know.

You know, she and I talked once about the death of my uncle Hollis. They had an open casket for his funeral. So much of my memory of him was in that casket. So much of the way I still visualize him is in that casket. He was like the first close person that I lost, before my dad died.

I always thought Nicole would be the person who would bury me. And I told her I didn't want an open casket. I didn't like the decision that was made with my uncle Hollis.

O.J.,

I pray every thing will work out for you and your beautiful children and your mom, dad, sisters, brother and any family you have.

*Everyone here in Texas
is pulling for you.*

*Mrs. Celeste Roberts
Pearland, TX*

Even before I bought my first home, I bought a home for my mother. I have two sisters and one brother. Shirley is my older sister, she works as a budget analyst in health care and she's been married for thirty-two years. She's more than just a big sister: Shirley was at times a mother. She is also totally spiritual, with "up" vibes. She's so positive about everything she is indestructible, the Rock of Gibraltar. Shirley would come in here and take my place if she could. That's Shirley. My mother did a hell of a job on her.

Carmelita, my other sister, is fiercely loyal, in many ways like me. She has always been a survivor and independent. She has a good job as an administrative executive, has always been responsible, and takes care of herself. She has been happily married for many, many years. She earned her way in life, owned her own home even before she got married.

Now my brother, Truman, he worked at a hotel until he retired and I always have to smile when I think of him. He's always joking that since I'm O.J., he's L.J. — Lemon Juice. But he's not bitter; he's never been bitter. He's always made people laugh. But he's fierce about telling everyone I'm his *little* brother.

Hi.

> *How are you today? O.J., you must be so proud of your son and daughter — Jason and Arnelle. I saw them on TV last week. Wonderful young people. So much more insight on you now. They should be on TV more often, and people will know you didn't do it.*
>
> *I'm listening to the 3 Tenors tape at Dodger Stadium — listen to it when you are low, especially "My Way."*

Stand Proud, O.J.

[Unsigned]
Postmark: Vancouver,
British Columbia

My kids Arnelle and Jason have matured so much through this experience. When I look at Arnelle, I see a lot of her mother, Marquerite. I don't think I could be any prouder of a kid than

I am of Arnelle. Her mother did a real good job. Marquerite deserves the credit. Arnelle has a cross section of friends, black and white, and Jason's girlfriend is mixed. When I look at my kids, I'm looking at evolution, social evolution. Arnelle originally had a thirst for living in a white neighborhood and then, with her black heritage, decided to transfer to a black college. It was good for her. She loved Howard University in Washington, D.C. Now she's a wardrobe consultant in L.A.

Jason studied some black history at one point. He's always been a great cook, and now he's an assistant chef. Jason did a family tree and it was really interesting watching him chart out the tree to see where we were from. He actually educated me, especially about my father's side of the family and the name Simpson. The Arkansas Simpsons were a white family and yet we adopted that name — that was the custom then.

I never saw myself getting married and having kids again. I was happy and I was content. Nicole and I got married because she wanted to have kids. We'd been living together for some six years then, and one day, she said she wanted to have kids of her own. She said: "I love kids and I want to have your kids." I loved her and I knew we could not have kids without getting married. My mom would never stand for that. I don't think Nicole would have stood for it either. I wasn't looking to get married. I had seen too many relationship that were great relationships until the people got married. I used to preach this to Nicole. I never wanted to hear the words:

"You're my husband," because before that she never said, "You're my boyfriend." We would both just say, "I love you." But I loved her and we got married.

Our wedding was a joyous affair. We got married outdoors at our home on Rockingham on February 2, 1985. Everybody was there, over 400 guests. There was so much love. Everybody was so happy for Nicole and me. She wanted it to be a celebration of our love for one another and I think it was. She made me a personal video depicting our seven years together and showed it during dinner. Nicole had monitors all over the place and people started crying looking at the video. It was done with so much love.

We never talked about how we were going to raise our kids. We never talked about our kids being interracial. We just said our kids were special. We lived in a neighborhood where a lot of people I know have interracial kids. Guys I played golf with, like Sidney Poitier, have interracial kids, gorgeous kids. Quincy Jones has interracial kids. We were around all these kids. So it wasn't an issue to us.

We were not the same after the kids were born, but we were happier in some ways. Nicole was manic, if that is the right word, about the kids. She never left them. To get her to leave Sydney for a weekend was impossible. She just loved being a mother. Sydney was so unusual looking, beautiful bronze skin with blond hair, that everybody would come up and say: "What a gorgeous kid." I would say to Sydney: "You're the best of Mommy and Daddy."

I love Nicole's family, the Brown family. We were an extended family. Their home was my home and ours was theirs. When Nicole's sisters needed help, I was there to help them. I believe in a good education and I helped Nicole's younger sisters, Dominique and Tanya, finance a better education when it was needed than what they might have had. Things have gotten a little out of hand with me and Nicole's sisters now that I have been accused of the murder of Nicole. I can understand some of it. I have no problem with Judy and Lou. Again, I say that in my most dire moments, when I was hurting the most, when I was totally frustrated in the years Nicole and I were together, I talked to Judy. So I could never have any animosity towards Judy and Lou Brown.

I will always want my kids to know Judy and Lou. Judy represents the spirit of Nicole, the spirit of caring that I loved in Nicole. Sydney and Justin should have all the contact they want, they need, with their grandparents.

Dear O.J.,

I think your friend Al Cowlings is the best friend anyone could ask for. His loyalty to you really touched me. You couldn't ask for a better friend. I have never met a friend like that in my life, and I envy you for having someone like him.

Love always,
Lesli Powell
Bakersfield, CA

Dear O.J.,

I also admire your friend Al Cowlings. That's a friend. You will know your friends by the ones who show up and stand by you when you are in trouble.

There's an old saying: "A friend is not a fellow who is taken in by <u>sham</u>. A friend is one who knows our faults and doesn't give a damn."

Delores A. Burke
Hyattsville, MD

I wish everybody had an A.C. in his life as a friend. Next to the word "friend" in the dictionary should be a picture of A.C. He has always had the biggest heart. A.C., like everyone, has had his problems in life — he has a temper — but nobody will ever question A.C.'s heart. He has goodness in him. I could go on and on. It was A.C. who brought my almost lifeless body back in his Bronco. I would never have survived that Friday if it had not been for him. That is all that needs to be said.

---

c/o O.J. Simpson

Dear Al Cowlings,

I cried when you were on the L.A. expressway. My heart was pounding, my palms were sweating and I was

screaming "Get away, O.J.," "Go, Al." I wanted O.J. to
be alive. You helped hold it together. You were the one
that enabled him to come back and defend himself.

When O.J. pleaded not guilty, I cheered. I was at my
university and people hugged each other and high-fived.
Yes, O.J. must stand by the truth!!!

Lovingly,

Valerie Lynn Stevens
Tallahassee, FL

I have felt bad that in recent years I haven't spent as much time
with my friend Robert Kardashian as I would have wanted to.
Robert, unknown to many, is a very spiritual guy. This guy has
never missed church, takes his kids to church every week.
Somehow even through all of this, he never misses church. He
and I lived together for a half year some time back. When
Robert split from his wife Kris, who is now Mrs. Bruce Jenner,
I didn't take sides. Even though Robert was my bosom buddy,
I tried to stay friends with Kris. I didn't hold the divorce
against her, and at one point, she came to me for advice. But
it's friends like Robert that I think I have taken for granted in
the past. It has become so clear who the goodhearted people
are — through thick and thin. Many people promote themselves as being a friend. Robert never did, but he is a true
friend. He is the person the world listened to on TV and radio

when he read my letter "To Whom It May Concern," on that Friday, June 17. There were things I wanted to explain, people I wanted to try to say goodbye to. The only person I could give my letter to was one I trusted, like Robert. He has told me that in his heart that day, he did not expect to see me alive again. Thank God for A.C. and Robert that I am here today.

Cathy Randa, my personal assistant, and I are probably as close as two people can be who have never been lovers. I don't think a sister and a brother could be closer than Cathy and I have been over the years. It's not like a mother and her daughter or a father and a son, where sometimes there's competition. I have shared with Cathy what I probably wouldn't share with almost anyone else.

I can't say enough about Skip Taft. He's been my business manager, my confidant, my adviser. I mean Skip has played every role that a dear friend can play in my personal and professional life. I trust Skip the way I trusted Nicole with the kids. I wouldn't question her and I don't question Skip. It's been over twenty years with both Cathy and Skip.

I felt uncomfortable about all my other material witnesses who are friends and who have stood by me. I have never been in the position of being a recipient. I've always been a giver. I'm not used to this and I've been thanking them too profusely. But I didn't realize that until they said: "Hey, Juice, it's easy." But still, thanks to Alan Austin, Joe Kolkowitz, Don Ohlmeyer, Bob Hoskins, Marc Reede, Marvin Channin, Craig Baumgartner, Bobby Chandler, Jack Gilardi, Joe Stellini, Peter

Locke, Peter Bort, Mark Slotkin, Marc Davidson, Allen Schwartz, Dino Buccola, Reggie McKenzie, Valerie and Erik Watts, and a special thanks to Nicole Pulvers. I'm sorry that I'm a burden on all of these people.

I was praying one night that God would send "Rosie" to talk and pray with you: The very next afternoon I switched channels just as "Rosie" was leaving the jail. Someone asked him what he'd talked about and he raised his Bible high in the air, and kept walking. I felt so good.

Give your mom my love when you communicate, and tell her sis. "Beth" is praying for her.

Love

Elizabeth Thomas
Miami, FL

When I was first arrested and put in jail, Rosie Grier came. I talked with Billy Graham too, but Rosie came first. He had some tough times in his life so he had been there, and he understood how I felt. At first he wanted me to learn the Bible. I have a belief in Jesus Christ, I have a belief in Heaven and Hell, I have a belief in right and wrong. But Rosie wanted to get into the real study thing. I was not into that. My head was someplace else. But what happened to me was I saw his enthusiasm.

Like others, it was good for Rosie to be here. The first two or three visits from Rosie, I think, did Rosie more good than me. To see this guy who at one point in his life was contemplating suicide too, and to see what the word of God meant to him, to see the enthusiasm that he had—bit by bit, it just became a sharing of his enthusiasm. He was glad.

Rosie was surprised at how much I knew about the Bible. He was shocked, in fact, at how much I knew, especially about Revelations and the other stuff I knew. In the beginning, he would be talking to me and I'd be half hearing him because I wasn't in a great place then. It was like Sunday school at the Evergreen Baptist Church. Finally, I kind of had to, in an inoffensive way, let Rosie know that I knew all about King David. But the zest he had became infectious. What you get from Rosie is goodness. It's the feeling that Rosie imparts.

I can tell you Rosie says the longest prayers of anybody I've ever known. He goes into a prayer and you've got to be sure to get comfortable, you've got to get all ready because it's going to be a while. Sometimes I literally got lost in his prayers. Sometimes I truly wander. In the middle of one of Rosie's prayers, I caught myself wandering. I had wandered off into one of my own prayers. Then I'd check back to see where Rosie was. But it's the love, it's the feeling, in some ways it's just the goodness he puts out. Rosie became for me a spiritual friend. He shared his feelings with me, he shared his spirit with me. Someday, when I am out of here, I will do the same with others.

Paula is my closest spiritual friend. Paula is a totally giving person. I have never been involved with a more giving person than Paula. She's devoted to God and she was raised to live by the Golden Rule. What else could I ask for?

Dear O.J.,

You should be proud that you've been able to help and support so many people and now it's time for them to do the same for you. People need to stick together in good and bad times and now you are going through a bad time so I hope if you get this letter it brings comfort to you knowing that so many people love and care about you.

Today so many people drop you as soon as they hear something negative about you and they don't stay around long enough to know if it's true or false.

God Bless You,

Kenya Shoffner
Greensboro, NC

A friend is someone who wishes you well, and I have to thank the thousands of people who have written to offer me their prayers, support, and kindness. The simple fact that they're writing helps, their prayers help. You can never have too many prayers going. To all those who wrote me, in a way you're my friends, friends I never knew I had. Thank you.

A little more than two weeks prior to Nicole's death, we had all these people at my home, parents and kids, enjoying what we had given to the community as a family. We had helped raise money for the school, and Nicole and I were lying together on the grass. Everyone who saw us said we were a loving couple and a giving couple with two great kids. Privately, we had reached a final decision not to go back together, a mutual decision. We were at peace with each other even though we were going down separate paths.

Once again Faye Resnick interfered in our relationship. She was one of the people I thought of as peripheral friends of Nicole who have turned out not to be any friends at all. These people, pretending to be respectable, are hindering my right to a fair trial with how they present themselves and their relationship to my family. As I've said, I have been totally unjudgmental of people all my life. It's a fault of mine. I now find it a fault.

I know in my heart that the answer to the death of Nicole and Mr. Goldman lies somewhere in the world that Faye Resnick inhabited.

Dear O.J.,

I do hope your two small children are not too frightened by the loss of their mother and the captivity of their father. I really feel for them and will keep them in my prayers for you.

Thanks, with Love for
You and Your Children,
Jacquelyn Lavine and friends
Castro Valley, CA

On November 21, 1994, I told Sydney and Justin that I was in jail and had been arrested for the death of their mother. They told me they already knew. Some of their friends had told them. They said they knew I was going to help find the people who killed their mommy.

Acknowledgments

O.J. Simpson determined to do this book, and provided essential access, cooperation, and time so that I could preserve his thoughts and feelings at this juncture. Rarely does one have the opportunity to sit with an individual when he is in the midst of the biggest battle of his life. It took a lot of courage for O.J. to sit for this portrait.

After concluding twenty-two hours of conversations, I shaped the interviews into book form and presented it to O.J. for his review. O.J. read the pages, made changes where he felt I had not understood the meaning of what he had said, and corrected facts, dates, and places. *I Want To Tell You* is O.J.'s spoken words in print.

I could not have written this book without the assistance of a great many people. First, I must thank the writers of the letters who, individually and cumulatively, provided the foundation for this book. The volunteers who read, and are still reading, the thousands of letters that O.J. receives each week are pictured at the end of this section.

David Johnston, of the *Philadelphia Inquirer,* a friend and colleague, joined me in California to assist. His work prepared me to enter O.J.'s world with the knowledge of the many thousands of letters addressed to O.J. As I conducted the interviews, David was there to discuss problems and to share opinions. David's contribution appears in many threads of this book.

Judith McNally, a good friend and occasional literary colleague, assisted me through the first draft, and her presence is here throughout the text.

Cathy Randa, O.J.'s personal assistant, contacted each correspondent whose letter appears in the book, and graciously thanked them for O.J. Cathy's contribution is also present everywhere in this book. O.J.'s housekeeper, Gigi Guarin, helped locate the personal photographs used in these pages.

Kathy Amerman has been at my side during this project, not only as a close friend, but as the photographer who photographed, for the publisher, all of O.J.'s volunteers, and some of the letter writers whose letters were used in this book.

I asked friends and family to read the first draft of this book before it went to O.J. I thank John Peters, Richard Moore, Pat Danova, my daughter, Suzanne, and my son Marc for their comments.

My personal staff included David Barron, Mark Dustrude, two fine professionals, and someone special, Andrea Kolb, who as deadlines loomed helped me to beat them. I also appreciate the technical assistance of Gary Randa, Amy E. Boyle Johnston, Marke Johnston, Tom Ruff, and Jim Troutman.

I am grateful to John Taylor "Ike" Williams, my valued attorney, of the Boston firm of Palmer and Dodge. Charles Hayward, the President and CEO of Little, Brown, had the vision that was needed for this book, and he provided the resources to enable me to complete the work in near-record time. Fredrica Friedman, Little, Brown's Executive Editor and Associate Publisher, brought her valuable experience, for what Fredi has forgotten about editing the written word would take two lifetimes to learn. A special thanks to the copyeditor and Little, Brown's chief book designer, who solved problems of layout and form with dispatch, and to my son Howard Schiller, who completed the production of the book in California. And to Icon West, Micro-rent, Martin Royer, and John Whitman for supplying technical equipment.

Lawrence Schiller
Los Angeles, California

Mail Volunteers

On the following pages are pictured the volunteers who sorted, categorized and read the 300,000 letters that were sent to O.J. since June 17, 1994. O.J. suggested that this picture be taken outside his home in Brentwood, California.

First row, kneeling, from left to right: Tim Kirk, Nancy Steinman, Patti Ganzar, Jerry Lucas-Churchill, Terri Baker, Judy Kawaguchi, Judy Ann Kulp, and Nicole Pulvers.

Second row, sitting: Delphia Edwards, Fumie Carrea, Ruby Everell, Val Perry, Charles Durio, Benny Baker, Shirley Baker, Madyson Baker, Gigi Guarin, Cathy Randa, and Arnelle Simpson.

Third row, standing: Ron Reynolds, Barbara Stockton, Denice Shakarian Halicki, Toni Baker, Joshua Baker, Wendy Fornaseri, Cynthia Mossiah, Tracy Baker, Carmelita Durio, Louise Perry, Jill Hall, and Jason Simpson.

Continued on page 204

Fourth row: Henry Kulp, Richard LaPaz, Christina Smith, Mary Anne Page, Laura Baker, Don Baker, Wesley Randa, Gary Randa, Matthew Randa, Dee Larrison, Caroline Lewis, Ramona Randa, Mary Collins, and Steve Lazarus.

Not pictured: Vicki Barnes, Barbara Carr, Shelly Coomes, Nancy Burchell, Peggy Coholan, Helen Swan, Karen Root, Sandy Montgomery, Joan Kipper, Ann Sullivan, Connie Linden, Julie Stockton, Lori Stockton, Eve Zinzell, Connie Lavine, Kathy Hudson, Sue Meyer, Cindy Bright, Gwen Tucker, Ruby Pitts, Bea Dunbar, Linda Gomez, Rochelle Metcalfe, Constance Arnick, Elizabeth Kiss, Rose Murphy, Ashley Cellar, Barbara Lorenz, Julie Steffes, Eunice Simpson, Jennifer Green, Nadia Tass, and David Parker.

O.J. Simpson Chronology

1947
> Born July 7th at San Francisco, Stanford U. Hospital.
> Parents Jimmie & Eunice Durden Simpson. Brother and sisters: Melvin
> "Truman" & Shirley older; Carmelita younger.

1949
> O.J. gets rickets.
> Mother makes home-made braces with bar. Worn to age five.

1958
> Sees Willie Mays play at Seals Stadium. Little League baseball game.

1959
> Nicole born in Frankfurt to Lou Brown and Juditha Bauer on May 19th.

1960
> Joins Persian Warriors gang in San Francisco.

1962
> Incarcerated for short period of time at S.F. Youth Guidance Center.

1964
> Meets Willie Mays.
> Is now playing baseball and football and running track.

1965
> Completes education at Galileo High, San Francisco.

1965
> Enters San Francisco City College.
> Gives up baseball, plays football and runs track.

1967
> Marquerite Whitley, age eighteen, marries O.J. on June 24th.

1967

Enters University of Southern California. Plays football to 1969.

1968

Wins Heisman Trophy award presented by the Downtown Athletic Club of New York City.

1968

Arnelle Simpson born to O.J. and Marguerite December 4th.

1969

Quits USC after 1968-69 football season ends.

O.J. purchases home for his mother. O.J. purchases his first home.

1969

1st draft pick Buffalo Bills in August.

Joins ABC Sports as commentator through 1977.

Chevrolet and RCA Cola spokesman through 1972.

1970

Jason Simpson born to Marguerite and O.J.on April 21st.

1974

Motion pictures *Towering Inferno* and *The Klansman*.

1975

Motion picture *Killer Force*.

National Football League Most Valuable Player.

Hertz spokesman to present.

1976

Montreal Summer Olympics commentator for ABC.

Dingo Boots spokesman to 1982.

Treesweet spokesman to 1983.

Hyde Spot-Bilt Athletic Industries spokesman to 1988.

Wilson Sporting Goods spokesman to 1989.

Advertising Age "Presenter of the Year" Award.

1977

Motion picture *Capricorn I*.

Ends Buffalo Bills career with 9,626 yards gained.

O.J. purchases his second home on Rockingham Avenue, Brentwood.

Aaren Simpson born to Marguerite and O.J. September 24th.

Meets Nicole Brown in June.

1978

Joins San Francisco 49ers on March 24th, plays for two seasons.
Motion picture *Firepower.*
Separates from Marquerite in October.
Joins NBC Sports as commentator through 1986.

1979

O.J. and Marquerite file for divorce in March.
Nicole Brown and O.J. date frequently after April.
Aaren Simpson drowns in pool on Rockingham on August 18th.

1983

Motion picture *Hambone & Hilly.*

1984

Commentator, Los Angeles Summer Olympics for NBC.

1985

Nicole Brown, age 26, married to O.J. Simpson at O.J.'s home on
    Rockingham on February 2nd.
Inductee Pro Football Hall of Fame.
Sydney Simpson born to Nicole and O.J. on October 17th.

1986

Joins HBO's *First and Ten* through 1989.
Jimmie Lee Simpson, O.J.'s father, dies.

1987

Arnelle Simpson graduates Crossroads High School.
Nabisco Brands spokesman to 1990.

1988

Motion picture *The Naked Gun.*
R. R. Donnelley & Sons Co. spokesman to 1991.

1988

Justin Simpson born to Nicole and O.J. on August 6th.
Jason Simpson graduates Army–Navy Academy.

1989

Nicole calls 911 on New Year's Eve.
O.J. gets community service from Judge Ronald.
Jason Simpson enrolls at USC.

_1991_

    Motion picture _Tipperary._

    Motion picture _Naked Gun 2 1/2._

_1992_

    Separation from Nicole on January 6th.

    Nicole files for divorce from O.J. on February 25th.

    O.J. meets Paula Barbieri in May.

    Arnelle Simpson graduates Howard University.

    Nicole divorced from O.J. on October 15th.

_1993_

    O.J. starts to date Nicole again in May.

_1994_

    Motion picture _Naked Gun 33 1/3._

    Nicole Brown Simpson murdered June 12th.

    O.J. Simpson arrested for the murder of Nicole and Mr. Ronald Goldman on June 17th.